POETIC YOUTH MINISTRY

POETIC YOUTH MINISTRY

Learning to Love Young People
by Letting Them Go

Jason Lief

CASCADE *Books* • Eugene, Oregon

POETIC YOUTH MINISTRY
Learning to Love Young People by Letting Them Go

Copyright © 2015 Jason Lief. All rights reserved. Except for brief quotations in critical publications or reviews, no part of this book may be reproduced in any manner without prior written permission from the publisher. Write: Permissions, Wipf and Stock Publishers, 199 W. 8th Ave., Suite 3, Eugene, OR 97401.

Cascade Books
An Imprint of Wipf and Stock Publishers
199 W. 8th Ave., Suite 3
Eugene, OR 97401

www.wipfandstock.com

ISBN 13: 978-1-4982-0243-5

Cataloguing-in-Publication Data

Lief, Jason.

    Poetic youth ministry : learning to love young people by letting them go / Jason Lief.

    xiv + 148 p. ; 23 cm. Includes bibliographical references and index.

    ISBN 13: 978-1-4982-0243-5

    1. Church work with youth. 2. Theology, Practical. 3. Postmodernism. I. Title.

BV4447 .L445 2015

Manufactured in the U.S.A.   03/18/2015

Scripture quotations are from the New Revised Standard Version Bible, copyright © 1989 the Division of Christian Education of the National Council of the Churches of Christ in the United States of America. Used by permission. All rights reserved.

To Naomi, Christian, and Savannah:
May your faith in Jesus bring a life of courage, joy, and love.

Contents

Foreword by Andrew Root | ix
Acknowledgments | xi
Abbreviations | xiii

CHAPTER 1
Vapor Trails: Young People Leaving the Church | 1

CHAPTER 2
Weakening Our Theology | 17

CHAPTER 3
The Pastoral Power of the Modern Social Imaginary | 33

CHAPTER 4
Failed Commodities | 55

CHAPTER 5
The Religious Problem | 71

CHAPTER 6
Faith, Youth, and the Task of the Christian Community | 89

CHAPTER 7
Conclusion: Poetic Youth Ministry | 117

Bibliography | 143
Index | 147

Foreword

I SAT IN THE back of the church wanting to somehow disappear into the cushion in the pew. It was confirmation Sunday, and one of the three confirmands in our little church was being confirmed. I had been his teacher for two years. And, filled with arrogance, I couldn't imagine he could have had a better teacher. After all, my day job is to teach pastors and youth workers across the globe how youth ministry is done, particularly with theological depth. So I confidently awaited this confirmand's five-minute presentation to the church, during which he would discuss what the person of Jesus meant to him as he confirmed his faith before the community. Yet, only a minute into his talk, I began questioning what I was doing with my life. There was little theological substance. Instead, after two years of deep discussion and reading Scripture together he could muster only platitudes about Jesus and so deeply relativized statements about faith and God that I wondered if I had violated the confirmation rite in allowing him to get this far at all.

Listening, I couldn't help but find myself caught in a cycle of shame that moved quickly and forcefully between the confirmand and myself. I found myself saying under my breath, "Kid, come on, can you really not think theologically?!" And then, "Man, what did I do wrong? What do I need to change; what strategy would work to get the results I want?" I moved back and forth from blaming young people to yearning like a thirsty man for water for the techniques that would get me the results I wanted.

I don't think I'm alone in this cycle, in this knee-jerk reaction to blaming the young and therefore seeking technical mastery of youth ministry to provide successful results. It feels like youth ministry has been stuck in a blame/technical mastery cycle since its congregational manifestation in 1970s. Even in many of our most important projects this cycle seems to show itself.

—Foreword—

Jason Lief has taken a bold step in this book to call you away from this cycle, using his significant academic mind like a hammer against the cycle, shattering it into pieces. He swings with such force that at times you'll be nervous; his very ability to wield the thoughts of Foucault, Charles Taylor, and others will, at times, lead you to fall back on your heels. But I hope you're brave enough to continue, for if you do you'll find within these pages a unique and very different take on youth ministry. Jason leaves no one safe in his deconstruction; significant voices in the field are exposed to the white-hot heat of his critique. And while I don't always agree with all of Jason's positions, I'm deeply impressed by his ability to step into intellectual and practical engagement. In these pages you're about to encounter a very talented philosopher, a thoughtful theologian, and a radically passionate pastor.

Ultimately what this book does for me, is remind me that the issues in youth ministry are much deeper and more beautiful than adolescent blame or technical procedures. Jason frees us from this cycle by showing us the philosophical problem of blaming young people and the theological bankruptcy of seeing faith as some kind of bag filled with skills of technical mastery. We so easily get ourselves stuck in this cycle because, as Jason beautifully shows, we have not taken into consideration enough how technocapitalism shapes our imaginations. I promise this book will rattle your cage, but, I believe, in the best of ways.

Andrew Root
Associate Professor and Carrie Olson Baalson Chair of Youth and Family Ministry, Luther Seminary

Acknowledgments

THE WRITING OF *POETIC Youth Ministry* is the culmination of seventeen years of teaching, coaching, and spending time with young people. The ten years I spent teaching high school forced me to think about the institutional world young people inhabit, but it wasn't until my time at Luther Seminary that I developed the theological language that helped make sense of the experience. Thanks to the guidance of excellent professors—Andrew Root, Theresa Latini, and Guillermo Hansen—I was able to bring the insights of theology, philosophy, and cultural theory into conversation with the issue of young people and Christian faith. This language was deepened through class discussions and arguments with my good friends and colleagues Patricia Abbas Abdelkarim and Peter Bauck.

The arguments and insights of this book were refined through many conversations at The Fruited Plain Café as well as the porches, decks, and sidewalks of my friends and colleagues. I am indebted to Mark Tazelaar for helping me better understand Bonhoeffer through a deeper appreciation of Nietzsche, and I'm grateful to Luke Hawley, Neal De Roo, Paul Fessler, Mark Verbruggen, and Walker Cosgrove for their encouragement and support. I'm also thankful to Dordt College for giving me the time and space to think through the ideas at the center of this project. Practically speaking, this book wouldn't have been possible if Helen and Lee Luhrs hadn't taken a trip to Germany, letting me spend a week at their beautiful home in Knoxville, Iowa, to read, write, and contemplate the meaning of life.

Finally, I'm grateful for the support of my family: my parents David and Sandy Lief, Gary and Nadine De Hoogh, my Uncle Rodney, who died too soon, but always made sure I put in an honest day's work, and my beautiful wife Tamara and our kids Naomi, Christian, and Savannah. This project would not have been possible without their patience, love, and support.

— ACKNOWLEDGMENTS —

Oh, and my kids would be upset if I didn't thank Lady, the most prayed for mutt in the history of canines, and valiant protector of the family home.

Abbreviations

DBWE 1	*Sanctorum Communio* (Dietrich Bonhoeffer Works English Edition)
DBWE 2	*Act and Being* (Dietrich Bonhoeffer Works English Edition)
DBWE 3	*Creation and Fall* (Dietrich Bonhoeffer Works English Edition)
DBWE 6	*Ethics* (Dietrich Bonhoeffer Works English Edition)
DBWE 8	*Letters and Papers from Prison* (Dietrich Bonhoeffer Works English Edition)
DBWE 16	*Conspiracy and Imprisonment* (Dietrich Bonhoeffer Works English Edition)
NSYR	*National Study of Youth and Religion*

CHAPTER 1

Vapor Trails

Young People Leaving the Church

THE FILM *WALL-E* TAKES place in a future where human consumption has trashed the earth, forcing people to live in spaceships while garbage-collecting robots clean the planet for future rehabitation.[1] As one particular robot named WALL-E (Waste Allocation Load Lifter Earth Class) goes about his work he collects cultural artifacts and stores them in his makeshift home. His most prized possession is a video recording of *Guys and Dolls* that plays in the background as he carefully organizes the day's haul: a spork, a Rubik's cube, and a lighter. At one point WALL-E stops to watch the TV, mesmerized as the characters hold hands and sing to each other. His gaze moves from the screen to his robotic hand. His obsession with human culture has awakened a form of consciousness, transforming a garbage-collecting robot into a relational, cultural being.

WALL-E's experience is in stark contrast to the humans living in space. Talking advertisements in the opening scenes tell a back story of human consumption and waste symbolized by the corporate power of Buy N' Large. The story eventually moves to a gigantic ship called the Axiom, where the temperature is always a perfect 72 degrees and humans float around on chairs as their needs are met by robots. While WALL-E has developed the humanlike capacities for work, culture, and relationships, the humans living on the Axiom are infantile and mechanistic. Unable to do anything for themselves, every activity—from eating, to playing, to moving from place

---

1. Stanton, "WALL-E."

to place—is done for them by machines. Incapable of social interaction, they communicate through screens. A giant sign reads "Welcome to the Economy" as advertisements displayed on the screens in front of them tell them what to wear and what to eat. They have no memory of earth or the way of life that once formed their identity as human beings.

At the center of this film is a question about human identity: What does it mean to be human? In many ways WALL-E is more human than the humans—he works, engages in cultural activity, and desires relationships. The humans, on the other hand, have become an abstraction. Enslaved to their machines, they live perfect lives in a perfect environment with no need for relationships or intimacy. They have "overcome" the earth, transcending their creaturely human identity for something "better" or more ideal. The story focuses on the tension between an abstracted humanity, content to live millions of miles away in outer space, and a garbage-collecting robot who awakens them to their humanity and brings them back down to earth.

A primary theme of *WALL-E* is the human ability to transcend or overcome every limitation through powerful techniques and processes. It is a quest for freedom fostered by a desire for an "ideal" world in which all limitations are overcome. This way of seeing the world emphasizes improvement and progress as a form of sanctification through which humans become better, improved, and successful—supported by systems and institutions that educate, nurture, form, and reform. Politics, economics, health care, and education become the social and cultural caretakers of what is considered "normal" and "ideal."

Increasingly, this represents the lived experience of young people in the West. As past stories and practices lose their authority, the way young people make meaning and construct identity is radically changed. No longer is identity something given, it is something that is constantly negotiated. The processes embedded within Western cultural institutions contribute to this by emphasizing discipline and improvement as the way to become ideal, successful human beings who positively contribute to society. This cultivates a desire for transcendence that creates an endless cycle of making and remaking identity in order to attain an ideal way of life. It is endless because it is impossible to attain; it is impossible because it is grounded in a view of humanity that is an abstraction. The result is a constant state of anxiety: the harder we try to attain it, the further we find ourselves from it. This is the world of the Axiom—the unattainable ideal human condition.

This reality became apparent to me when I was asked to speak at a local youth gathering. I was asked to address the issue of identity so I began with the question: What does it mean to be human? To get the discussion started I used a clip from *WALL-E* that shows WALL-E first arriving on the Axiom. As the scene played everyone laughed at the ridiculous portrayal of hyper-reality that showed humans floating on chairs, talking through screens, and acting like helpless infants. When the scene ended I asked, "What went through your mind as you watched this clip?" Instantly a young woman blurted out "Dude! That's totally us!" causing the whole group to laugh, nodding their heads in agreement. "Really?" I responded. "So, what are you going to do about it?" I asked. "Oh, nothing," she replied.

In a matter of moments this group of young people experienced both recognition and resignation. They recognized their social and cultural life as it played on the screen, and many of them realized how ridiculous it looked. Yet, they also recognized the tight grip this way of life has upon how they imagine the world. They admit that it is problematic, but they have resigned themselves to the fact that they are not going to do anything about it.

This response to *WALL-E* reveals the complex issues at work in the current problem of young people leaving the church. As young people make meaning and construct identity they do so living within powerful social and cultural structures that offer a competing vision of the higher good and what it means to be human. Increasingly, as the research shows, young people find this alternative view of the world to be much more convincing.

What's Happening?

In 2012 the Pew Forum on Religion and Public Life released the findings of a recent study that explored the religious commitments of Americans. The report, "'Nones' on the Rise: One-in-Five Adults have No Religious Affiliation," found that the number of Americans who claim no religious belief has risen 5 percent in the last five years from 15 percent of the population to 20 percent of the population.[2] For this study the term "none" was used to refer not only to people who claim no religious affiliation, including those who self-identify as atheists and agnostics, but also to a number of participants who claim some form of spirituality but do not identify with

---

2. Pew Forum, "'Nones.'"

traditional forms of religion. Much of the growth in this category comes from people under thirty. According to the report:

> The growth in the number of religiously unaffiliated Americans—sometimes called the rise of the "nones"—is largely driven by generational replacement, the gradual supplanting of older generations by newer ones. A third of adults under 30 have no religious affiliation (32%), compared with just one-in-ten who are 65 and older (9%). And young adults today are much more likely to be unaffiliated than previous generations were at a similar stage in their lives.[3]

Similarly, David Kinnaman, author of the book *You Lost Me: Why Young Christians are Leaving the Church and Rethinking Faith*, reports that roughly three out of five young Christians (59 percent) are "disconnecting" from the faith sometime between adolescence and their late twenties and thirties.[4] Kinnaman writes:

> The ages eighteen to twenty-nine are the black hole of church attendance; this segment is "missing in action" from most congregations. . . . The percentage of church attendees bottoms out during the beginning of adulthood. Overall, there is a 43 percent drop off between the teen and early adult years in terms of church engagement. These numbers represent about eight million twentysomethings who were active churchgoers as teenagers but who will no longer be particularly engaged in church by their thirtieth birthday.[5]

A 2007 LifeWay Research survey suggests that 65 percent of young adults who attended church as teenagers stopped attending for at least a year between the ages of eighteen and twenty-two.[6] For Kara Powell and Chap Clark, the authors of the book *Sticky Faith: Everyday Ideas to Build Lasting Faith in Your Kids*, this supports their claim that at least 40 to 50 percent of

---

3. Ibid.

4. Barna Group, "Six Reasons." For a critique of Barna research methodology, see Johnson and Stark, "Bad News Bearers," and Wright, *Christians are Hate-Filled Hypocrites*.

5. Kinnaman and Hawkins, *You Lost Me*, 22.

6. Gallup, "The Religiosity Cycle." See also LifeWay Research, "Church Dropouts." See also Martinson, Black, and Roberto, *Spirit and Culture*. This book summarizes the research findings of the Exemplary Youth Ministry Study.

young people "who graduate from a church or youth group will fail to stick with their faith in college."[7]

Finally, "The National Study of Youth and Religion (NSYR)," a longitudinal study that explored the religious experience of young people, reported a significant change in the religious participation of young people as they move through adolescence.[8] In his book *Souls in Transition: The Religious and Spiritual Lives of Emerging Adults*, Christian Smith describes how close to 40 percent of the young people who participated in the five-year study demonstrated a noticeable decline in religious belief and practice.[9] This data shows that adolescents have a hard time articulating their beliefs, and when they do it tends to take the form of what he calls Moral Therapeutic Deism. Smith summarizes it this way:

> The creed of this religion, as codified from what emerged from our interviews with U.S. teenagers, sounds something like this:
>
> 1. A God exists who created and orders the world and watches over human life on earth.
>
> 2. God wants people to be good, nice, and fair to each other, as taught in the Bible and by most world religions.
>
> 3. The central goal of life is to be happy and to feel good about oneself.
>
> 4. God does not need to be particularly involved in one's life except when God is needed to resolve a problem.
>
> 5. Good people go to heaven when they die.[10]

---

7. Powell and Clark, *Sticky Faith*, 15. See also Hill, "Faith and Understanding." Hill writes, "There is no straightforward effect of college on religious beliefs. . . . However, this does not mean that college has no impact on belief. The results do suggest that belief in super-empirical entities and occurrences are altered for some students as a result of attending and graduating from college. The effect is particularly pronounced for those attending elite universities. There is a detectable decline in both conventional Christian super-empirical beliefs as well as super-empirical beliefs related to non-Christian traditions (although Christian super-empiricism exhibits the greatest decline because of higher education). Students on America's college campuses are not abandoning Christian beliefs and adopting other religious beliefs. Rather, there appears to be a modest tendency to become skeptical of the existence of super-empirical entities and occurrences generally." "Faith and Understanding," 545–46.

8. National Study of Youth and Religion.

9. Smith and Patricia Snell, *Souls in Transition*.

10. Smith and Denton, *Soul Searching*, 162–63.

Smith acknowledges that the data reveals a diverse religious experience among young people; however, the study also found that the religious belief system most common among American adolescents is not a traditional version of Christian faith.[11] Smith writes, "Moralistic Therapeutic Deism may not simply be what an ill informed or nominal faith sounds like in a teen interview. It may be the new mainstream American religious faith for our culturally post Christian, individualistic, mass consumer capitalist society."[12]

Finally, the NSYR suggests that the best indicators of adolescent belief and practice are the religious beliefs and practice of their parents.[13] This is significant because it shows that contrary to the more popular view of adolescence as a time of rebellion and differentiation, parents and adults play an essential role in the way young people form religious beliefs and practices. At the same time, the fact that Moral Therapeutic Deism is the default belief system of adolescents raises important questions about the beliefs and practices of adults. Smith writes, "Contemporary teenagers have almost entirely bought into the mainstream social system, literally anxious above all to succeed on its terms. They are well socialized to want to enjoy the consumerist and experiential benefits of U.S. society as much as they are able. Most problems and issues that adults typically consider teenage problems are in fact inextricably linked to adult-world problems."[14]

Smith's most recent work focuses on the third phase of the NYSR, in which he interviewed the same group of young people five years later as they became adults. In *Lost in Transition: The Dark Side of Emerging Adulthood* Smith argues that the religious confusion that marked the period of adolescence, symbolized by the prevalence of Moral Therapeutic Deism, shows up in "emergent adulthood" as a lack of commitment to religious belief.[15] Smith argues that the rapid social and cultural changes over the last few decades have disrupted the usual processes of moral and religious formation. Smith writes, "Emerging adulthood tends both to raise the stakes on and remove social support for being seriously religious. As a

---

11. Ibid., 262.
12. Ibid.
13. Ibid., 261.
14. Ibid., 264.
15. For more information on "emergent adulthood" see Arnett, *Emerging Adulthood*.

result, many youth do pull back from, or entirely out of, religious faith and practice during their transitions out of the teenage years."[16]

The response of the Christian community to this situation tends to focus on two areas: strengthening the beliefs and practices of the Christian community, and making the gospel more culturally relevant. The first approach frames the issue as a theological problem in which churches have abandoned orthodox teaching while watering down Christian practices. The solution, then, is for churches to refocus attention on a faithful interpretation and communication of the gospel tradition by reclaiming forms of Christian practice that help young people develop a meaningful Christian faith and identity. While cultural engagement is important, it serves a secondary function by providing the context in which the tradition is interpreted and lived out.

An example of this approach is Kenda Creasy Dean's *Almost Christian*. Dean uses the data from the NSYR research along with the work of Christian Smith to argue that the primary issue affecting the religious beliefs of young people is the presence of Moral Therapeutic Deism in our churches. The blame for this, however, should not be placed on young people but on the adults. Dean writes:

> The most plausible explanation is more insidious. Even if teenagers participate fully in youth ministry programs, are involved in churches, and manage to dodge disruptive life events and overwhelming counter influences, youth are unlikely to take hold of a "god" who is too limp to take hold of them. Perhaps young people lack robust Christian identities because churches offer such a stripped-down version of Christianity that it no longer poses a viable alternative to imposter spiritualities like Moralistic Therapeutic Deism. If teenagers lack an articulate faith, maybe it is because the faith we show them it too spineless to merit much in the way of conversation. Maybe teenagers' inability to talk about religion is not because the church inspires a faith too deep for words, but because the God story that we tell is too vapid to merit more than a superficial vocabulary.[17]

For Dean, the problem of young people leaving the church is directly related to the fact that adults have replaced orthodox Christian beliefs and practice with "niceness" and "compliance." She argues that the church is

---

16. Smith and Snell, *Souls in Transition*, 283.
17. Dean, *Almost Christian*, 36.

reaping what it has sown, as we receive "from teenagers exactly what we have asked them for: assent, not conviction; compliance, not faith. Young people invest in religion precisely what they think it is worth—and if they think the church is worth of benign whatever-ism and no more, then the indictment falls not on them, but on us."[18]

To address this, Dean suggests a strategy that focuses on reclaiming a missional focus of the gospel. This is an approach to Christian identity grounded in beliefs and practices that shape members of the community as they imitate Christ.[19] She provides three principles to guide these practices: the indigenizing principle (translation), the pilgrim principle (discipleship), and the liminal principle (decentering practices). Together, these principles constitute an emphasis on interpretation and discipleship that continually calls for the community to provide fresh interpretation and new practices for every historical and cultural context. By grounding the belief and practice of the community in a biblical and theological understanding of God's mission in the world, Dean argues that Moral Therapeutic Deism will be rendered powerless and young people will be connected to the deep life-giving tradition of the Christian community.

The importance of Dean's perspective is that it frames the problem of young people leaving the church in the context of the beliefs and practice of the Christian community. Adolescents and emergent adults are not inherently opposed to religion; the real problem, according to Dean, is that they are being initiated into Moral Therapeutic Deism, and this is the reality that the Christian community must now deal with as young people officially cut ties with traditional forms of the Christian faith.

The second approach focuses on the relationship between the Christian community and contemporary Western culture. This argument takes the position that young people are leaving the church because the Christian community refuses to address significant cultural changes that have taken place over the last fifty years. For many young people the church is giving answers to questions that they are not even asking, while it is closed off to the pressing cultural issues young people are now faced with. The consequence of this cultural gap is that young people increasingly find Christianity to be outdated, preferring the world view offered by science, economics, and the broader culture, and this is why they are leaving the church. Those who hold this position insist that the church must take the issues and

---

18. Ibid., 37.
19. Ibid., 70.

questions of the broader culture much more seriously by accommodating the tradition to the questions and issues of contemporary Western culture.

An important voice for this argument is David Kinnaman, author of *You Lost Me: Why Young Christians are Leaving the Church and Rethinking Faith*. Using Barna research from the *You Lost Me* project, Kinnaman argues that young people are leaving the church because of the growing disconnect between their rapidly changing cultural experience and the beliefs of the Christian community. Kinnaman refers to this as "disciple-making gaps," which he explains using the terms *access, alienation,* and *authority*.[20] "Access" refers to the changing technological reality in which young people have access to an overwhelming amount of information and entertainment, changing the way they think about the world. These new forms of technology have produced a rupture between traditional ways of life and contemporary practices, creating tension between the way past generations have viewed the world and the new ways that "mosaics" construct meaning and identity.[21] This has carried over into the beliefs and practices of the church, as these new forms of technology and science have called into question the way Christians have engaged cultural issues. A significant problem facing the Christian community is the perception that it is not responding quickly enough to this technological transformation and the consequences it has had upon the way young people understand meaning and identity.

"Alienation" describes the relational disconnect that exists between what he calls the "mosaic" generation and the "boomer" generation, stemming from these cultural changes.[22] This cultural shift has dramatically affected the way young people participate in the realms of politics, the media, and institutions, establishing a growing divide between how older and younger generations experience the world. Kinnaman writes:

> The Mosaic generation is skeptical, even cynical, about the institutions that have shaped our society, and while they retain an undiminished optimism about the future, they see themselves creating that future mostly disengaged from (or at least reinventing) the institutions that have defined our culture thus far. Few institutions in our culture are immune to the impact of the next

20. Kinnaman and Hawkins, *You Lost Me*, 39.
21. Ibid., 41.
22. Kinnaman defines "Mosaics" as "those born 1984 through 2002; many of today's teenagers and twentysomethings, often referred to as Millennials or Gen Y. Barna Group uses Mosaic because it reflects their eclectic relationships, thinking styles, and learning formats, among other things." Ibid., 246.

generation—from music to media, from the workplace to education, from politics to the church. The generational churn at play within the religious establishment is, in many ways, part and parcel of the alienation affecting every segment of our society.[23]

Closely related to this issue is the transformation in the way young people understand the issue of "authority." Kinnaman argues that young people are inherently skeptical of authority, which extends to their religious experiences and how they view the role Christian belief plays within cultural life. Kinnaman writes, "Questions about the proper role of faith in politics, sexuality, science, media, technology, and so on are simply being reframed to avoid debate—making people of faith irrelevant to the conversation. . . . There is a sense, across the board, of benign apathy toward Christianity."[24]

Like Dean, Kinnaman argues that the broader cultural and social changes have had a negative effect on the religious beliefs and practices of young people. The formative power of the broader culture plays a significant role in shaping the way young people think about religious belief and practice. Without a substantive response by the Christian community to these cultural changes, the credibility gap between the cultural experience of young people and the Christian community is maintained. The lack of intentional response by the Christian community to the shifting cultural experience of young people is, for Kinnaman, the primary reason why young people are leaving the church.

The significance of Kinnaman's work is that he takes the lived cultural experience of young people very seriously. He recognizes that the beliefs and practices of the Christian community need to address the rapidly changing cultural experience of young people, and that the problem of young people leaving the church presents an opportunity to focus on this cultural divide by finding ways to bridge the gap of social and cultural change.

Closely related to Kinnaman's work is *Sticky Faith: Everyday Ideas to Build Lasting Faith in your Kids,* by Kara Powell and Chap Clark, which explores practices for congregations and families to help faith "stick" with young people as they transition to college life. Powell and Clark agree with Smith's assessment that most young people have a difficult time articulating what they believe. When asked "What would you say being a Christian is all about?" many participants in the College Transition Study (two-thirds) focused upon what the authors refer to as "external faith"—good works,

23. Ibid., 50.
24. Ibid., 53.

spiritual disciplines, etc.[25] The authors also found that young people tended to respond with a list of "do's" and "don'ts."[26] The premise of *Sticky Faith* is that this "external" understanding of faith does not stick; therefore, the Christian community must develop practices to cultivate an "internal faith," which the authors articulate as a form of "trust." They write, "So as a general rule, when we see the words faith or belief in the Bible, they come from *pisteuo* and thus can be translated as 'trust.' As you help your kids understand Sticky Faith, every decision, every thought, and every action comes down to this: in whom do I place my trust?"[27]

The primary focus of *Sticky Faith* is to show the difference between salvation by "works" and an understanding of faith as "trust." The problem with "works," according to the authors, is that they remain external, while "trust" is internal and becomes the bond that makes faith stick. This does not eliminate the need for external forms of practice; instead, it forces the community to search for practices that help cultivate an internal "trust" in Jesus Christ.

The goal of *Sticky Faith* is to help the Christian community develop strategic practices that build inward trust to form a faith that sticks. The practices they suggest range from how to respond to a child who "misbehaves," to building relationships, to creating experiences that instill a sense of service and justice. Building off of the work of Dallas Willard, *Sticky Faith* describes the problem of young people leaving the church as a failure of the community to develop practices that form and shape an inward faith (trust) that is strong enough to withstand the transition from home to college life.

Sticky Faith addresses one of the most significant points of transition in the lives of young people in the West: the move to college. As Christian Smith describes in his analysis of emergent adulthood, one of the primary changes that has taken place over the past century has been the extension of adolescence through the expansion of higher education. Because this formative period is usually spent away from the traditional support systems for religious belief and practice (family and church home) young people are left to develop religious practices and habits on their own. In recognition of this transitional stage of life, *Sticky Faith* offers parents and churches

---

25. Powell and Clark, *Sticky Faith*, 33.
26. Ibid., 34.
27. Ibid., 35.

practical advice on how to help young people make this transition and find a supportive church community.

The recurring theme found throughout this literature is that the Christian community has either failed to cultivate the right practices that ground the identity of young people in orthodox Christian belief, or the community has failed to seriously engage the new cultural reality young people inhabit every day. This failure has opened the door for a generic, secularized, belief system—Moral Therapeutic Deism—that mirrors the values of the broader culture. For these authors the Christian community has failed to cultivate moral formation, orthodox belief, and a relevant cultural engagement, which has resulted in young people leaving the church for other forms of community and religious experience.

A Powerful Social Imaginary

There is much about these approaches to the problem of young people and the church that is insightful and helpful. It is important for the Christian community to develop a deep biblical and theological understanding of the Christian tradition that speaks to how God is at work in the world. It is also important for the church to continually reinterpret the tradition for new and different cultural contexts as we lovingly and courageously engage the cultural issues young people are facing. What is missing, however, is an exploration of the powerful hold these social and cultural patterns have over the imaginations of young people. Often the social and cultural world young people inhabit is seen as secondary to the beliefs and practices of the traditions, either as the medium through which the Christian tradition is communicated or as the questions the gospel must answer. But the cultural world young people inhabit is not just a set of social, institutional, or linguistic conditions to be addressed; it is a way of life built upon a "social imaginary" that intends the world to be a certain way. These cultural and social patterns establish a meaningful way of being in the world that forms and shapes the way young people experience the world.

This is why it is important to explore the formative religious function of the social and cultural patterns. In *WALL-E*, for example, there is a religious function to the Axiom that shapes a social imaginary—or prerational world view—that signifies the ultimate meaning and highest good. The issue is not just that humans float on chairs, talk to each other through screens, or buy things with the push of a button; the deeper issue is that the social imaginary of the Axiom shapes the way humans make sense of the world. The same is true for the cultural experience of young people in the West. The cultural institutions and patterns are not just the context in which young people exist, or the medium through which they communicate—they also shape the imaginations of young people so they experience the world in a certain way that determines meaning and a sense of the highest good. Including this in the discussion of why young people are leaving the church allows the Christian community to frame the issue properly: young people are not abandoning religious belief; they are exchanging one form of religious belief for another.

It is important to recognize how the Christian community and social imaginary of Western culture offer competing visions of faith and faith formation. The social imaginary of Western culture is increasingly shaped by a new vision of economic life—global technocapitalism—that emphasizes progress, surplus value, and the transcendence of humanity through technological processes.[28] This new cultural situation cultivates a cycle of desire for an ideal (abstract) human identity through the formation of institutions and social patterns as it generates its own vision of salvation, sanctification, and eschatology, which is communicated through new rituals and practices. Salvation, in this context, is articulated in the language of economic abstraction—wealth, improvement, growth, and progress—that is undergirded by the rhetoric and practices of social and cultural institutions. Together, these practices and institutions establish a vision of human identity that is grounded in the norms and values of global technocapitalism that works to shape the imagination and identity of young people.

Just as important is the ability of the global technocapitalist world view to co-opt the practices of the Christian community for its own purposes. As the church responds to the issue of young people leaving the

---

28. *Global technocapitalism* is a term that signifies the drastic shift in the socioeconomic situation of the West during the late twentieth and early twenty-first centuries. This shift is a move away from an industrial, hierarchical form of capitalism into a corporate, network-based capitalism in which the primary resources are knowledge and creativity. The catalyst for this form of capitalism is the development of new technologies that allow for the growth of a global economy. Suarez-Villa defines technocapitalism this way: "Technocapitalism is defined in this book as a new form of capitalism that is heavily grounded on corporate power and its exploitation of technological creativity. Creativity, an intangible human quality, is the most precious resource of this new incarnation of capitalism. Corporate power and profit inevitably depend on the commodification of creativity through research regimes that must generate new inventions and innovation." *Invention and the Rise of Technocapitalism*, 10.

church by developing new processes of faith formation and cultural engagement they risk being co-opted by the global-technocapitalist world view. Much of the Christian language is easily translated into a secular paradigm in which "salvation" becomes focused upon human flourishing through wealth, well-being, and happiness. Similarly, processes of spiritual and moral improvement become interchangeable with processes of social or economic improvement and well-being. Taken further, it is easy to see how young people make the jump from a Christian understanding of salvation and sanctification to a secularized faith of progress and well-being. Thus, the spiritual and moral improvement offered in Christianity is easily exchanged for the improvement and progress young people encounter in athletics, school, and other cultural activities.

To address this it is important for the church to clarify what it means when it talks about faith. While much time is spent talking about faith, and developing new processes of faith formation, less time is spent clarifying exactly what we mean when we talk about faith. An important part of the response to the issue of young people leaving the church must include a biblical and theological description of the object of Christian faith—the crucified and risen Jesus Christ who is the revelation of divine action in the world, and the word spoken about what it means to be a human creature living in relationship with God.

At the same time, it is important to recognize the object of faith undergirding the religious function of global technocapitalism in Western society in order to help the community become aware of the processes, techniques, and practices at work in the lives of young people. This helps the Christian community better understand how the global capitalist paradigm is able to co-opt the processes and practices of the church, which contributes to young people exchanging Christianity belief for the secularized religion of global technocapitalism. Recognizing this religious function helps the community to frame the problem correctly, not as the abandonment of faith, but the exchange of one form of faith (Christian faith) for another (global technocapitalism). Once the problem is framed in this way, then the Christian community is in a better position to provide a response.

Letting Go

Which leads to the question explored in this book: *What if the proper response to the problem of young people leaving the church is to let them go?*

By "let them go" I do not mean to abandoning young people, or letting them do whatever they want. What I mean is that the Christian community should engage this issue by practicing a weak theology grounded in the revelation of God and humanity in the death and resurrection of Jesus Christ. "Weak theology," which comes from the theological and philosophical work of John Captuo and Gianni Vattimo (weak thought), interprets the cross of Jesus Christ as a deconstructive and subversive expression of love. For Caputo and Vattimo the gospel is not about asserting strong theological principles of absolute truth as a form of power or control; the point is not to make sure young people act a certain way or hold specific beliefs. It's not even about trying to keep young people in the church. Instead, weak theology sees the gospel as a force that loosens or deconstructs every attempt to name or categorize the world. It frees individuals and communities to finally encounter the neighbor and the world in freedom and grace. Ultimately, weak theology declares the coming of a kingdom that does not categorize or exclude, but is a kingdom that is "of base, ill-born, powerless outsiders who are null and void in the eyes of the world."[29]

Responses to the current issue of young people leaving the church tend to be driven by fear and anxiety, often asserting a strong theological response that emphasizes doctrinal beliefs or processes and procedures. Processes of faith formation and discipleship tend to focus on measurable moral, theological, or cultural outcomes. The problem with this approach is that it closely mirrors the global technocapitalist paradigm that establishes norms and procedures—directed toward an ideal form of human identity—which distinguish insiders (those closest to the ideal and thus the most desirable) from the outsiders (those who fail to live up to the norm). While doctrinal beliefs and faith formation are an important part of the Christian community, this type of strong response runs the risk of being co-opted by the dominant ideology.

A response grounded in a weak theology directly challenges the technocapitalist emphasis on control, management, and commodification. It runs contrary to the global technocapitalist networks of insiders and outsiders that are marked by performance and desirability, subverting every attempt to abstract human identity by affirming the finite, vulnerable, creaturely experience of being human. A weak theological response throws a wrench in the gears of global technocapitalism, refusing to play by its rules

---

29. Caputo, *Weakness of God*, 48.

by inviting young people to experience their finite human identity in the crucified and risen Christ.

This book will explore a weak theological response to young people leaving the church in three parts: The first will explain the difference between a strong theology and weak theology using the work of John Caputo and Gianni Vattimo in relation to the formative power of Moral Therapeutic Deism as the strong theology of global technocapitalism. Using the philosophical work of Michel Foucault and Charles Taylor, I will explore the rise of the modern social imaginary and the pastoral power imbedded within the social and cultural institutional life. Taylor's work will help explain how this historical shift signifies a new religious paradigm embedded within the techniques and practices of economic and political life. Finally, I will examine the experience of young people living within the contemporary social patterns that "pastorally" form and shape the identity of young people.

The second part will focus on a biblical and theological articulation of Christian faith in the theological work of Dietrich Bonhoeffer, specifically focusing on his articulation of a "religionless Christianity" as a critique of Moral Therapeutic Deism and the way global technocapitalism violently categorizes and abstracts the lives of young people. This section will explore how Bonhoeffer's interpretation of the death and resurrection of Jesus Christ points to the true identity of God and humanity that calls young people into a new way of life grounded in the new humanity of Jesus Christ. By responding to this issue out of a posture of love, the Christian community provides a counternarrative to global technocapitalism and its tendency to abstract the identity of young people in the name of an "ideal" humanity attained through constant technological and economic improvement.

The final section will provide guidelines for the Christian community as it addresses the lives of young people and calls them to a human life of courage and responsibility grounded in the new humanity of Jesus Christ. This chapter will articulate a vision for a "poetic" or a "weak" form of youth ministry that counters the abstraction and fragmentation of technocapitalism by helping young people construct an identity grounded in a faith in the crucified and risen Christ. In this form of youth ministry the youth pastor and youth leaders function as "interpretive guides" by helping young people "remythologize" or renarrate the world in the context of the revelation of God in Jesus Christ.

Chapter 2

Weakening Our Theology

WHENEVER I USE *WALL-E* in a youth group setting I tell everyone to pay attention to the lines. There is not much dialogue in the film—very little is said during the first twenty minutes—but if you pay close attention the images have much to say. The world of the Axiom is a world of lines that creates order and establishes a controlled, predictable, way of life. Until, of course, WALL-E comes aboard.

Prior to WALL-E's arrival on the Axiom, he becomes infatuated with a robot named EVE (Extraterrestrial Vegetation Evaluator) who has come to earth to find signs of life. When he tries to impress her with a green plant in an old boot it triggers a series of events that sends WALL-E and EVE to the Axiom with its world of lines. As WALL-E weaves in and out of traffic trying to keep up with EVE he accidently knocks a human named John out of his chair. With the line impeded, traffic comes to a standstill as John lies helplessly on the ground. Eventually, security robots come and draw new lines around John that allow traffic to resume. No one stops to help; they are instructed to "wait" for a service robot to arrive. WALL-E assesses the situation. Propping John back up into his chair, he introduces himself, and continues on his way.

As he moves through the ship WALL-E passes children sitting in lines, learning the alphabet by reciting Buy N' Large propaganda. A voice over the loudspeaker instructs everyone to "try blue, it's the new red," and with the push of a button everyone's bodysuit changes from red to blue. Life on the Axiom runs smoothly because everything has its place, and everyone knows his or her role. More importantly, everyone does what they are told, and they always follow the lines.

Later in the story, while trying to retrieve the boot plant, WALL-E is jettisoned out of the Axiom in an escape pod set to self-destruct. Seconds before it explodes he uses a fire extinguisher to punch open the hatch. EVE, who thinks WALL-E has exploded, is overjoyed when he shoots past, riding the fire extinguisher. What follows is a beautifully poetic scene in which WALL-E and EVE fly together outside of the Axiom in a playful dance of curved lines. Music plays as WALL-E and EVE joyfully fly in and out of various structures on the Axiom, juxtaposed with the voice of the captain as he asks the computer to define dancing.

These two scenes contrast the human life on the Axiom with the relationship between WALL-E and EVE. The Axiom is a mechanistic world of straight lines where everything is confined to a set of rules. WALL-E and EVE, on the other hand, inhabit the human experience of playful relationships, beauty, and grace. In fact, WALL-E and EVE function as a sign to the humans on the ship, reminding them of what they were meant to be and how they were meant to live. John, who WALL-E helped back up onto his floating chair, and a woman named Mary, watch out the window as WALL-E and EVE dance through space. When they both recognize WALL-E they accidently touch each other's hands, a spark of intimacy that reminds them of their humanity.

Strong Theology: Building the Kingdom

The contrast between the lines of the Axiom and the poetically curved lines of WALL-E and EVE's dance symbolizes the difference between a "strong" and "weak" response to young people leaving the church. The focus of "strong" theology is to exercise power by using language to make positive statements about God, the kingdom of God, and the way the world should be. In strong theology doctrinal and theological statements are taken to have an objective correlation to the nature of God and God's being, which influences how God's action in the world is understood. At the same time the Bible tends to be read in such a way that the words and language are taken as the objective truth about God, humanity, and the world. What I mean is that there is a strong correlation between the language (the sign) and that to which the language is pointing (the referent.) Simplistic examples of this include the use of the male pronoun for God, the ethical admonitions of Paul, or a historical and scientific approach to the creation accounts. The truth of doctrine or the Bible in this context is grounded in how it correlates to historical, scientific, and cultural reality.

When applied to ministry and discipleship strong theology becomes the foundation for a triumphalistic posture as the Christian community makes metaphysical claims about God, humanity, and the world. The kingdom of God is associated with a particular way of life grounded in particular doctrinal and moral principles, while salvation is framed in the context of giving assent to specific beliefs about God and holding to specific ethical positions. While grace and faith are still the primary ways to speak of God's salvation in Jesus Christ, they eventually give way to doctrinal beliefs and ethical positions that mark the members of the Christian community. In this context salvation is seen as the saving of people from the world by bringing them into the kingdom of God. Much of the language associated with the task of the Christian community emphasizes "spreading" or "building" the kingdom of God. Ultimately, a strong theological approach seeks to separate, establishing lines that mark the insiders from the outsiders. While all of this is couched in the language of loving the world, it is accomplished by bringing the world into the kingdom of God, which means bringing it into a certain way of life marked by believing certain doctrinal and ethical principles.

Holding on Too Tight

This discussion provides an important window into the problem of young people leaving the church. When understood through the lens of strong theology this phenomenon becomes a crisis precisely because young people are stepping outside the lines—moving from being insiders to being outsiders as they abandon the beliefs and practices that distinguish them from the world. The anxiety and fear this brings causes the church to resort to a strong theological response by trying to help young people believe doctrinal propositions by using new techniques and approaches. Practices of faith formation and discipleship are seen as a way to help make sure these beliefs stick. Often, attempts are made to adapt to the church to the broader culture through a change of worship styles or church structures, while mission or service projects become a strategy to ensure young people are putting their beliefs into practice.

This strong theological approach can be seen in the field of youth ministry, which seems to exist in a perpetual state of crisis. Added to this is the anxiety and fear surrounding the issue of young people leaving the church. For some, youth ministry is part of the problem—it segregates young people into separate programs and communities, disconnecting them from what it means to be the church.[1] For others the lack of seriousness that has characterized youth ministry has fostered a superficial understanding of community and faith, forcing young people to look elsewhere for a serious exploration of meaning and identity.[2] At the same time, much time and energy has been dedicated to describing the interests, needs, and experiences of young people to help congregations relate to the lives of young people and emerging adults.[3]

Others appeal to a strong biblical or theological emphasis in an attempt to refocus youth ministry in response to this crisis. In his book *Jesus-Centered Youth Ministry: Moving from Jesus Plus to Jesus Only*, Rick Lawrence sees the problem as a lack of a biblical center in youth ministry, arguing that youth programs need to reclaim a focus on helping young people understand who Jesus is. He writes:

> All of our conventional responses to this steamrolling crisis have missed the mark. We've tried to become more relevant, more glitzy, more tolerant, more technologically savvy, more flexible, more professional, more sophisticated, more purpose-driven, more comprehensive, more socially aware, more . . . more. But all of our "mores" have done nothing to reverse the trend of disengagement. Even though there are more highly trained, fully resourced youth workers than at any other time in the church's history, the youth ministry landscape looks bleaker than ever before. The evidence is telling us that, despite our best efforts, today's teenagers just aren't getting who Jesus really is. And that's the biggest problem . . .[4]

Lawrence argues that the Christian community needs to change its focus from strategies and techniques so they can help young people rediscover or re-encounter Jesus. He sees youth ministry as a place where adults can help young people learn to abide in Jesus so they might have the principles of

---

1. For an example of a critique of age-segregated youth ministry, see Alvin L. Reid, *Raising the Bar*.

2. See White, *Practicing Discernment with Youth*. See also Senter, *Four Views of Youth Ministry*.

3. See Mueller, *Youth Culture 101*, and Clark, *Hurt 2.0*.

4. Lawrence, *Jesus-Centered Youth Ministry*, 6.

the kingdom of God implanted in their lives. The focus of youth ministry should be to help young people answer two questions: "Who do I say Jesus is?" and "Who does Jesus say that I am?" Every question and issue—every passage of Scripture—must be brought back to Jesus.

The practices that shape the ministry of the church to young people must constantly bring young people back to Jesus. Lawrence suggests that every lesson should connect back to the question of the identity of Jesus, and those experiences of mission and evangelism should put young people in situations where they are forced to depend upon the power and authority of Christ's Spirit. He argues that youth ministry must tell the truth about Jesus, which means introducing them to the "dangerous" Jesus, and that it should focus on the "red stuff"—the words of Jesus highlighted in red in certain Bible translations.[5]

The Jesus that Lawrence wants young people to encounter in youth ministry is a strong, dangerous Jesus, grounded in a strong form of theology that lays claim to a specific way for young people to know Jesus through the Bible and experience, while the "red-letter" approach reveals an objective view of the Bible that implies a direct correlation between what is written in red and what Jesus actually said. This can also be seen in the three-question strategy that is recommended for the study of the Bible. There, lessons focus on asking: What did Jesus really say? What did Jesus really do? How did people really experience Jesus?[6]

Here, the use of the word "really" suggests a strong correlation between the words of Scripture and the metaphysical reality of Jesus and the world in which he lived. This becomes the foundation for the techniques and practices that determine the true way of the kingdom of God, or a true form of ministry and discipleship, from those that are misguided. The author is right to suggest that youth ministry needs to move away from a works-oriented understanding of faith formation and ministry that replaces Jesus with techniques and formulas; however, we have to be careful that we do not end up creating a new magic formula around the name of Jesus and the Bible.

What *Jesus-Centered Youth Ministry* gets right is that youth ministry needs to have Jesus as the center of its belief and practice. What this looks like, however, is what differentiates a "strong" theology from a "weak" theology. It's possible that the call to focus on Jesus can become an abstraction

---

5. Ibid., 51.
6. Ibid.

that is never given theological content. The beeline concept that insists everything must connect to Jesus can end up short-circuiting the complexity of the incarnation and hermeneutical task of the community. To say that nothing else matters but Jesus, if taken to its logical conclusion, can be taken to mean that, in the end, Jesus doesn't matter. If Jesus is cut off from the cultural life of young people, where they construct a human identity, then it is possible to say that Jesus really doesn't matter for daily, ordinary, life. A weak theological view of the incarnation, on the other hand, flips this around as the death and resurrection of Jesus Christ weakens or negates the radical transcendence of strong theology, so that the opposite is true—in Jesus everything matters.

Building and Growing Faith?

A number of youth ministry books invoke the strong theological language of "building."[7] Whether it's building the kingdom, building youth programs, or building disciples, the default response to the current issue of young people and faith is to construct. Often, the language of building and growing is applied to faith, suggesting that there is some objective blueprint or plan that youth leaders and congregations can use to construct young people who will have a strong faith and commitment to the church.

This is supported by language of "growth" and "development" and a view of ministry that sees salvation as bringing young people out of the world and into the Christian community. This establishes an "us versus them" paradigm in which the purpose of the church, and the purpose of youth ministry, is to make sure young people remain community insiders. As we will see, this language is easily co-opted by the global technocapitalist paradigm with an emphasis upon growth, production, and improvement, as well as the creation of a well-defined network of insiders and outsiders.

In *Sticky Faith* the authors encourage parents and youth workers to develop practices that help young people learn to "trust in Jesus" rather than focus on a works-oriented form of "sin management." The strong language of "building" provides the metaphor for helping young people develop a faith that will stick when they leave for college. Even though the intent is to move away from a works emphasis they emphasize markers that differentiate those who have true faith from those who do not have faith.

---

7. Robbins, *Building a Youth Ministry*.

—Weakening Our Theology—

This can be seen in the story about Tiffany, a young woman who becomes pregnant out of wedlock. The purpose of the story is to give a concrete example of someone who was once a vibrant member of the Christian community, but who eventually dressed differently, left youth group, became pregnant, and lost her faith. The authors write, "Why did Tiffany's faith—a faith that seemed so vibrant at first—fail to stick?"[8] The assumption is that Tiffany's clothing, choice of makeup, and unplanned pregnancy function as indicators of her lack of Christian faith. Here we can see the fear and anxiety that young people who are part of the community might end up leaving and become outsiders, making it important to develop practices that will build a faith that will stick.

David Kinnaman, in *You Lost Me*, also uses the language of building and production in response to the cultural disconnect he sees affecting the church. Kinnaman argues that the church needs new "architects" to build "new ecosystems of spiritual and vocational apprenticeship that can support deeper relationship and more vibrant faith formation . . ."[9] He emphasizes that the Christian community in the West is at a "critical point" and that the church must reexamine how it thinks about discipleship within this new cultural reality that young people inhabit. For Kinnaman, this crisis in discipleship means the Christian community must be willing to rethink the issue of faith formation and discipleship by building new institutions, relationships, and networks of power and influence, all for the sake of reaching young people who are leaving the church.

These examples demonstrate the tendency of the Christian community to respond to young people leaving the church by asserting a strong theology. The constant use of terms like "build" and "grow" suggest an exercise of power through processes and practices that form the faith and identity of young people. This exercise of power makes important assumptions about the nature of the gospel and the kingdom of God. It assumes that the kingdom of God is metaphysical, that is has a particular content that directly correlates to doctrinal and ethical principles, and that the objectivity of the kingdom means that there is building and growing to be done. It assumes that the kingdom of God is divisive—that it has come to separate insiders from outsiders. It assumes that the death and resurrection of Jesus Christ is about the assertion of sovereign power that establishes a militant kingdom in the world.

8. Powell and Clark, *Sticky Faith*, 15.
9. Kinnaman and Hawkins, *You Lost Me*, 13.

This is the form of strong power that is used to address the issue of young people and faith. If the kingdom is metaphysical, if it's about establishing an identity of insiders and outsiders, then the doctrines and principles of this kingdom become important tools to form and shape the lives of young people. Here we see how faith formation becomes about "building" and "growing" disciples, and practices and procedures become about the production of faith and identity that sticks with young people. As with the symbolic world of the Axiom, practices of faith formation and discipleship become the procedures—the straight lines—that bring order and control to the construction of Christian identity.

I admit that for many in the Christian community it might be difficult to see why this type of response is a problem. Clearly, one can find biblical and theological support for this approach, and it makes sense in the context of practical theology and youth ministry. However, as I will try to demonstrate, there are significant problems with using this posture to respond to the issue of young people leaving the church.

Not of This World: The Weakening Force of the Kingdom of God

Biblically, a "strong theology" contradicts Jesus' own understanding of the kingdom of God. When confronted by Pilate, Jesus replies by saying, "My kingdom is not from this world. If my kingdom were from this world, my followers would be fighting to keep me from being handed over to the Jews. But as it is, my kingdom is not from here" (John 18:36). In John's gospel the word *world* can refer to two things: the created world and the patterns that govern the world. Jesus' response to Pilate invokes the second reference. Jesus is not saying that the kingdom of God is some spiritual, otherworldly kingdom; he is saying that the inner working of his kingdom is not like Pilate's kingdom. Where Pilate's kingdom—Rome—was dependent upon the use of strength, violence, and force, Jesus insists that his kingdom is fundamentally different.

This same message is found in Paul's proclamation of the weakness and foolishness of the cross. Paul writes, "But we proclaim Christ crucified, a stumbling block to Jews and foolishness to Gentiles. . . . For God's foolishness is wiser than human wisdom, and God's weakness is stronger than human strength" (1 Cor 1:23–25). John Caputo, in his book *The Weakness of God: A Theology of the Event* writes,

> When human rule is displaced by the rule of God, foolishness is favored over the Sophia and philosophia of the present age (aion).... Those whom God calls upon are not wise, not powerful, not well-born (eugeneis).... That is the key to what is called the kingdom of God in the Synoptics: God chose the "outsiders," the people deprived of power, wealth, education, high birth, high culture. Theirs is a "royalty" of outcasts, so that, from the point of view of the aion, the age or the world, the word kingdom is being used ironically, almost mockingly, to refer to those pockets of the despised that infect and infest the world. For this is a kingdom of the low-down and lowborn, the "excluded," the very people who are precisely the victims of the world's power.[10]

The gospel in this context is an "event" that deconstructs and subverts every attempt to name, to control, and to build. It is opposed to every form of absolute Truth and every claim to certainty. This connects with what Paul says to in his Letter to the Galatians, "There is no longer Jew or Greek, there is no longer slave nor free, there is no longer male nor female; for all of you are one in Christ Jesus" (3:28). These categories were the cultural categories upon which identity in the ancient world was to be built. For Paul, the death and resurrection of Jesus Christ blew these categories up, so that no longer did they legitimately have any power to name or control. Paul goes on to tell the Galatians that they are free, "So you are no longer a slave but a child, and if a child then also an heir, through God" (Gal 4:7).

For Gianni Vattimo, the purpose of the gospel is not to construct a kingdom of absolute objective truth; the purpose of the gospel is not to establish new cultural markers that delineate insider from outsider. Instead, the gospel proclaims a message of charity that weakens and subverts every cultural power that tries to name, to identify, and to control—every power that attempts to build and organize in the name of absolute Truth. Vattimo writes,

> The truth that, according to Jesus, shall make us free is not the objective truth of science or even that of theology: likewise, the Bible is not a cosmological treatise or a handbook of anthropology or theology. The scriptural revelation was not delivered to give us knowledge of how we are, what God is like, what the "natures" of things or the laws of geometry are, and so on, as if we could be saved through the "knowledge" of truth. The only truth revealed to us by Scripture, the one that can never be demythologized in

---

10. Caputo, *Weakness of God*, 46.

the course of time—since it is not an experimental, logical, or metaphysical statement but a call to practice—is the truth of love, of charity.[11]

For Vattimo, the gospel does not take people out of the world, it doesn't seek to divide humanity into insiders and outsiders. Instead, it frees the world—frees humanity—to live as a playful kingdom of love. This is the gospel that young people need to hear.

Many of the authors above would agree, arguing that they too are concerned with issues of identity, sin, and the salvation revealed in Jesus Christ that frees humanity from every false god. The problem, however, is that they are not content to allow the gospel to deconstruct; many in the Christian community want to build new structures and processes, constructing an objective Christian reality that names and defines. They develop objective processes to make sure that young people grow in faith and become disciples. They establish new cultural boundaries of "in" and "out" that mark faith from unbelief. The intention is good; undoubtedly, it is done out of love and concern for young people and faithfulness to the gospel. The problem is that this building of the kingdom necessarily involves establishing new power structures, new lines of demarcation, and new systems of control. What is most problematic about this new building project is that is so easily co-opted by the dominant ideology of the West, global technocapitalism, and its new religion—Moral Therapeutic Deism.

Identity, Culture, and Christian Faith

A crucial aspect of the issues that shape the way young people experience religious belief is the way in which identity and meaning is mediated through the symbols and ideologies of the broader social and cultural world. While many acknowledge the negative influence the broader culture has upon young people, they believe that the Christian community can overcome this influence by creating new forms of ministry and practice. The contemporary social and cultural world is understood to be the arena in which the Christian community addresses young people; it is the language, institutions, and way of life to which the gospel must be applied so that young people can hear the saving message about Jesus Christ. In this

---

11. Vattimo, *After Christianity*, 50–51.

context youth ministry must include cultural engagement as the gospel is interpreted and translated into every cultural context.

What is often overlooked is how the cultural world young people inhabit provides the linguistic and mythic tools for young people to make meaning of the world. These cultural tools—language, symbols, institutions, and ideologies—are not just the context in which the Christian tradition is received and interpreted; these cultural forms inscribe themselves upon the tradition, which means there is no objective or pure hearing of the gospel; it is always an ideological reception of the tradition. When it comes to the problem of young people leaving the church, the Christian community fails to recognize the profound influence the technocapitalist ideology has upon the way young people experience religious belief and practice.

Furthermore, because the language of faith formation and discipleship tends to be similar to the technocapitalist language (growth, building, producing, etc.), it becomes very easy for young people to move from one form of religious belief (Christianity) into the secularized religious paradigm of global technocapitalism. An important part of this problem is a lack of definition or clarity regarding what it means to have faith in Jesus Christ. Many of the authors discussed above provide a very thin understanding of faith and discipleship, focusing much more on the processes and practices needed to grow or develop faith and identity. This thin description unintentionally contributes to the religious confusion that leads to the pervasive influence of "Moralistic Therapeutic Deism." Without a thick theological and biblical understanding of faith and discipleship, the practices of faith formation, regardless of the intention, can become religious processes focused on transcending the human condition as the language of salvation and sanctification become religious attempts to be "good" or "better." Becoming like Jesus, keeping Jesus at the center, or trusting in Jesus—which at face value make sense—end up promoting anxious attempts to improve, to become moral, to become more biblical or doctrinal, all as marks of discipleship or proof of faith. This leads to important questions about the relationship between divine and human action. Is "faith" something that can be produced or grown? Or is faith something that must be given, an event that transcends human consciousness and human categories?

Because the Christian tradition is received and interpreted within the context of the global technocapitalist ideology of contemporary Western society, every attempt to address the issue of young people and faith through the development of new processes runs the risk of being co-opted by the very paradigm it tries to prevent. The cultural lives of young people are saturated with the language of progress, improvement, and growth. Capitalism provides its own narrative of transcending ethnicity, gender, and class to create a better life. The institutions young people inhabit support this view of life: educational institutions, athletics, economics, the arts, etc. all reinforce the religious ideology of Western culture by focusing on procedures and processes as the way to ideal humanity.

As the church takes its place among the institutional voices addressing the lives of young people, the issue of young people leaving the church is given context. The language of faith formation and discipleship in many ways parallels the technocapitalist emphasis upon improvement and progress, causing the Christian view of salvation and sanctification to be conflated with the religious ideology of Western culture. Ultimately, however, young people find the Christian narrative of salvation to be archaic, an antiquated approach to human flourishing that doesn't line up with cultural reality. As a result, young people exchange the belief and practice of orthodox Christianity for the belief and practices of global technocapitalism—putting their faith in economics and technology to improve their lives and lead them to the eschatological vision of flourishing grounded in wealth, production, and technological solutions to global problems.

The problem with the current responses to this issue is that they fail to engage this cultural reality. Without a thick description of the meaning of faith and discipleship, the practices of the community leave young people susceptible to the pervasive religious function of global technocapitalism. For the Christian community to address the issue of young people leaving the church it must unmask the formative ideological power of contemporary social and cultural patterns in the West, while at the same time providing a clear articulation of the object of faith for the Christian community. Doing this will help to properly frame the problem of young people leaving the church as a conflict between competing versions of faith: Moral Therapeutic Deism and global technocapitalism versus orthodox Christianity.

The Religious Function of Western Society

In order to provide a thick description of the religious and pastoral function of contemporary Western society, and the pervasive hold it has on the imaginations of young people, it is important to establish the historical and philosophical conditions that led to the development of this social and institutional way of life. Just as important is an understanding of the modern social imaginary, and how it frames the way young people meaningfully make sense of the world and their identities as human beings living in the world. An important place to begin this discussion is with the work of Charles Taylor.

In *The Secular Age* philosopher Charles Taylor describes the conditions that gave rise to the world of modernity and the fundamental belief that human nature and identity have the capacity to be "transformed." For Taylor, this development is deeply connected to the pastoral power and spiritual discipline of the church during the middle ages. He argues that the period of reform during the sixteenth century broke down the separation between church life (spiritual) and cultural life (temporal), which unleashed pastoral power into everyday cultural life as a form of "sanctification of the ordinary."[12] Taylor puts it this way:

> It has two facets: it promotes ordinary life, as a site for the highest forms of Christian life; and it also has an anti-elitist thrust: it takes down those allegedly higher modes of existence, whether in the Church (monastic vocations) or in the world (ancient-derived ethics which place contemplation higher than productive existence). . . . Both these facets have been formative of modern civilization. The first is part of the background to the central place given to the economic in our lives, as also for the tremendous importance we put on family life or "relationships." The second underlies the fundamental importance of equality in our social and political lives. All of these factors, material and spiritual, help explain the gradual promotion of the economic to its central place . . . The notion becomes more and more accredited that commerce and economic activity is the path to peace and orderly existence.[13]

Taylor argues that this new religious emphasis upon the sanctification of ordinary life placed a higher value on the economic and political spheres that provide the basis for modernity and the rise of capitalism. While some within the Christian community strongly oppose what they refer to as "secularism" and "consumerism," Taylor argues that the secular, economic focus of modern culture has its roots in the religious reforms of the sixteenth century.[14] He describes how by the eighteenth century the hope for a

---

12. Taylor, *Secular Age*, 179.

13. Ibid., 179–80.

14. For two different views on "secularization theory" see Löwith, *Meaning in History*, and Blumenberg, *Legitimacy*.

good life, as well as the definition of the good life, is deeply connected with forms of politics and economics that represent new forms of "pastoral" or disciplinary power embedded within new social patterns and institutions. As we'll see more clearly in the next chapter, Taylor sees contemporary Western society as being comprised of social and cultural patterns that serve a pastoral function: forming the imaginations and identities of individuals according to the new economic and political realities of capitalism.

So what does this have to do with the problem of young people leaving the church? Taylor argues that the development of modern institutional life, the rise of the secular, and the pervasive influence of global capitalism, are fundamentally religious developments. He demonstrates that the "object of faith" for this way of life is a belief in an immanent "god" that is present in the natural laws and ordering of the world. Through the presence of "god" in the structures and ordering of society, humanity is empowered to transcend the difficulties of material life by creating new forms of peace, security, and "happiness" through the political and economic spheres of ordinary life.

This takes place through the pedagogy of institutional life as individuals are "disciplined"— meaning they are deconstructed and reconstructed—in a way that allows them to improve and transcend their material conditions. While much of this religious language has been lost, describing secular life using religious or spiritual terms helps us to see the pastoral function of Western culture as it seeks to form identity and meaning through economic and political practices.

This articulation of the pastoral function of Western culture provides a way to reframe the problem of young people leaving the church. To talk about young people leaving the church, or even orthodox Christianity, does not mean that young people have lost faith. Instead, the issue is more appropriately framed as the exchange of one form of faith for another. This move from Christian faith to a secular way of life is best interpreted as the exchange of one view of "salvation" for another. Young people increasingly see the capitalist narrative as a more plausible and effective form of belief and practice for overcoming "sin." To put it simply, young people are leaving the church because the capitalist "gospel" is much more believable to them than the one being offered by the church.

This is supported by many of the responses given by young adults in Christian Smith's research on emergent adulthood. When posed a question about the possibility that mass consumerism represents a distortion of "spiritual life," one young adult responded by saying:

> They're probably right. But at the same time I guess this is one place where I'm just like, "This is the world we live in, either get on board or be unhappy." I don't really know what to tell you. I guess I really don't agree with people who are like, "Let's go granola." That's really unnecessary. You don't have to live that way anymore. You have the opportunity to live better. That's why your parents did what they could for you, and their parents did for them, is to give you this. We are improved. Be improved.[15]

Another responded this way:

> It feels good to be able to get things that you want and you work for the money. If you want something, you get it. It makes your life more comfortable and I guess it just makes you feel good about yourself as well. You want to get some, you work for it and you can get it. I think it's a good thing to buy what you want if you work for it, because when you work for something, then you gain that accomplishment. . . . It's like you actually work for that thing so you feel that you deserve it, you earned it.[16]

And another said this:

> Okay, when I'm having a bad day, a bad week, whatever, there is nothing that makes me feel better about myself more than going and buying myself a whole new wardrobe. I feel like a better person . . . I feel more intelligent sometimes, I feel cleaner, it's just a great feeling. I feel self-sufficient 'cause I bought it on my own.[17]

Every response has a religious overtone focused on personal transformation through the act of consumption. Smith addresses this by writing, "Here we find a vision for self-improvement, for growth and transcendence beyond the old. But the improvement in this case does not concern self or morals or social justice, but rather material lifestyles and personal consumption."[18] He summarizes the issue by writing, "So what is the horizon of mainstream American culture today? In America's current 'cultural ontology,' what is taken to be ultimately real and what therefore ought to be prized and

---

15. Smith et al., *Lost In Transition*, 72–73.
16. Ibid., 73.
17. Ibid., 74.
18. Ibid., 73.

sought after? Could it be the triumph of liberal democratic capitalism has erased from the common American imagination any higher, transcendent horizon?"[19]

The response of the Christian community to the problem of young people leaving the church must begin with an articulation of "faith": in what, or in whom, do we believe? This must be a two-pronged approach that clarifies the object of Christian faith while also clarifying the "object of faith" of the broader social and cultural praxis. Doing this will help to clarify the current issue of young people leaving the church as a competition between two expressions of faith with two very different articulations of sin, salvation, and what it means to be a human being. This clarification will empower the community to cultivate practices that are directly related to the object of Christian faith, while at the same time they problematize the ideological influence of global technocapitalism.

The following chapters will focus upon providing a description of the cultural situation of young people in the West living in the West. Beginning with an engagement of the work of Charles Taylor, as well as Michel Foucault, I will demonstrate the pastoral function of the institutions within contemporary Western society, while connecting this pastoral function to the "salvific" power of global technocapitalism.

19. Ibid., 236.

CHAPTER 3

The Pastoral Power of the Modern Social Imaginary

IF THE CONNECTION BETWEEN the story of *WALL-E* and the lived experience of young people living in the West isn't clear, then let me be more explicit: I believe the cultural world young people inhabit in the West is the world of the Axiom. The utopian mechanistic world of lines symbolically represents a world of control and management; a world in which human identity is carefully and subtly directed towards an ideal established by the norms of the Axiom. In a similar way, the cultural and institutional life of young people in the West subtly guides them toward the ideal humanity demarcated by the norms of global technocapitalism. These norms establish the insiders from the outsiders, the successfully adjusted from the delinquents, the ideal life marked by wealth, possessions, and technology, from an abnormal failed life.

The spatial symbolism in *WALL-E* is important as humans abandon the earth to live in outer space on the Axiom—a name that refers to abstract principles and objective truth. WALL-E functions as a "foreign contaminant"—the label given to him by a cleaning robot named MO (Microbe Obliterator)—because he is a garbage compacting robot more at home on earth than outer space. The plot centers on the conflict between AUTO, the Axiom's autopilot, who wants to protect the utopian life of the Axiom, and WALL-E and EVE, who are trying to help humanity return to earth. AUTO and the Axiom symbolize the overcoming of a material, creaturely life through techniques and processes; it is a place where humanity lives as an abstraction: humans don't work, they don't struggle or suffer, they don't have meaningful relationships. They live within a virtual reality of utopian consumption.

To properly address the problem of young people leaving the church it is important to recognize the ways in which the world of the Axiom represents the experiences of young people living in the West. They inhabit social and cultural institutions that disconnect them from their creaturely, material existence, forcing them to inhabit new economic cycles of production and consumption. Under the pervasive influence of global technocapitalism young people are forced to construct and reconstruct an identity that others will find desirable, turning themselves into commodities to be consumed in a never-ending cycle of technological and economic abstraction. To put it differently, young people are forced to meet the ever-changing expectations of the adult world by making something of themselves. Whether it is in education, entertainment, employment, or the church—young people want to make themselves desirable, consumable, and therefore normal. This is the Axiom experience.

But how did it come to this? What are the historical and philosophical forces that have shaped this new reality, and how has this had a dramatic impact upon the religious beliefs of young people today? An important place to start is by exploring the rise of modernity and the pervasive influence of secularity.

The Religious Function of the Secular Age

In *A Secular Age*, Charles Taylor traces the rise of secularity from the late middle ages, through the Enlightenment, and into the present. His primary focus is to show how the development of the secular society in the West dramatically affected religious belief and practice with the rise of atheism. Taylor writes, "the change I want to define and trace is one which takes us from a society in which it was virtually impossible not to believe in God, to one in which faith, even for the staunchest believer, is one human possibility among others."[1] He goes on to write, "Belief in God is no longer axiomatic. There are alternatives. And this will also likely mean that, at least in certain milieu, it may be hard to sustain one's faith. There will be people who feel bound to give it up, even though they mourn the loss."[2]

---

1. Taylor, *Secular Age*, 3.
2. Ibid.

The Pastoral Power of the Modern Social Imaginary

Taylor explores how the changes in religious belief can be attributed to significant cultural changes over the past 500 years. He focuses on the period of the Reformation and how it dramatically disrupted the "background framework" or "social imaginary" that shaped the way people thought about God and cultural life, establishing the groundwork for the cultural, philosophical, and religious changes that led to modernity and postmodernity.[3]

But how does this help us make sense of the religious experience of young people in the West? The remainder of this chapter will focus on Taylor's argument that the Reformation was the catalyst for cultural and religious changes that made certain forms of religious belief more difficult, while creating the conditions for new forms of belief to emerge. It is the secularizing forces of this shift that will help us make sense of young people leaving traditional forms of Christianity. As a part of this exploration we will examine Michel Foucault's arguments regarding the "disciplinary society" that have embedded new forms of pastoral power within the structures and patterns of modern society. All of this has established the conditions that allowed capitalism to become the dominant force within Western society, culminating in the current manifestation—global technocapitalism—and Moral Therapeutic Deism.

Changing Beliefs: The Rise of Secularity

Primarily, Taylor's *A Secular Age* is his attempt to answer a question about the cultural conditions of religious belief. He writes, "One way to put the question I want to answer here is this: why was it virtually impossible not to believe in God, in say 1500 in our Western society, while in 2000 many of us find this not only easy but even inescapable?"[4] Taylor is interested to describe the historical and cultural changes that led to the secularization of Western society and the possibility of "unbelief." The social imaginary of the 1500s provided the conditions for an enchanted view of the world in which meaning resided in forces and subjects outside the human mind. The human person was viewed as a "porous self," which meant that there were "things" and "agencies" outside of the self that influenced human identity, as the supernatural impressed itself upon human experience.[5] Because the

3. Ibid., 13.
4. Ibid., 25.
5. Ibid., 40.

natural world was believed to be capable of mediating the supernatural, a sacramental system developed in which the divine was mediated through physical objects like bread, wine, water, and the relics of the saints. The social and cultural patterns of the time were grounded in a belief that reality is permeable, meaning the natural and supernatural mixed together, which helped create a hierarchical society that shaped the identities of individuals and communities.

Within this "enchanted" social imaginary "God" became the foundation for social order. Taylor writes, "The social bond at all these levels was intertwined in the sacred, and indeed, it was unimaginable otherwise. . . . And so, this utterly solid and indispensable reality argues for God. Not only does it follow: I have moral and spiritual aspirations, therefore God is; but also: we are linked in society, therefore God is."[6]

Unbelief, in this context, is not an option because the entire social fabric is based upon the mediation of the supernatural through the natural. This social and cultural reality made unbelief almost impossible. Truth and identity are not constructed; they are given from somewhere "out there," forming the imaginations of individuals and entire communities in such a way that to deny belief in God would mean the collapse of the entire social arrangement.

The Reformation is important, for Taylor, because it begins a process of radical transformation in which this view of the world was dismantled through a movement of double disenchantment. He writes:

> The energy of disenchantment is double. First negative, we must reject everything which smacks of idolatry. We combat the enchanted world, without quarter . . . [T]he second energy was positive. We feel a new freedom in a world shorn of the sacred, and the limits it sets for us, to re-order things as seems best. . . . We are not deterred by the older tabus, or supposedly sacred ordering. So we can rationalise the world, expel the mystery from it (because it is all now concentrated in the will of God). A great energy is released to re-order affairs in secular time.[7]

For Taylor, the Reformational disenchantment of the world disconnected the supernatural from the social and cultural patterns, making the radical reordering of society possible.

---

6. Ibid., 43.
7. Ibid., 80.

An important part of Taylor's argument is that this impulse of reform, with a focus upon inward piety, the disenchantment of religious practice, and the glorification of God through vocation and the ordinary life, corresponds with the development of the "disciplinary society." In response to the perceived social disorder of the time, the impulse of church reform in the sixteenth century brought with it an emphasis upon the moral transformation of society through the exertion of discipline: a new form of monastic asceticism directed at the ordering of the ordinary life.[8] Taylor summarizes the move towards social reform this way:

> There are certain common features running through all these attempts at reform and organization: (1) they are activist; they seek effective measures to re-order society, they are highly interventionist; (2) they are uniformizing: they aim to apply a single model or schema to everything and everybody; they attempt to eliminate anomalies, exceptions, marginal populations, and all kinds of non-conformists; (3) they are homogenizing; although they still operate in societies based upon differences of rank, their general tendency is to reduce differences, to educate the masses, and to make them conform more and more to the standards governing their betters. This is very clear in the church reformations; but it is also true of the attempts to order people's lives by the "police states"; (4) they are "rationalizing" in Weber's double sense: that is, they not only involve an increased use of instrumental reason, in the very process of activist reform, as well as in designing some of the ends of reform . . . but they also try to order society by a coherent set of rules . . .[9]

As the church reforms of the sixteenth century spilled over into the realm of social reform, they made possible the shift to a Cartesian world view. As the natural world became disconnected from the supernatural, the sacramental view of nature was replaced by a view of the world as raw materials for humans to rationally control and manipulate. Instead of an enchanted view in which humanity is formed and shaped by outside forces, the divine was increasingly viewed as an internal experience that empowered personal and social transformation.

According to Taylor, this shift from an enchanted social imaginary to a Cartesian version created the necessary conditions for what can be called "exclusive humanism" in which the highest good of society is no longer the

---

8. Ibid., 82.
9. Ibid., 86.

supernatural, but human flourishing. He traces this development from the Enlightenment, through the nineteenth century declaration of the death of God, into contemporary Western society. While the social imaginary of the 1500s left very little room for unbelief, the developments of the eighteenth and nineteenth centuries established the conditions for a social imaginary that made belief in God much more difficult. Thus, it is this shift in social imaginary, sparked by the religious and cultural reforms of the sixteenth century, that has made religious belief much more problematic within the contemporary Western world.

The Immanent Frame

This dramatic shift in social imaginary is, for Taylor, the lens through which the significant issues regarding religious belief within contemporary Western society must be examined. Through this process of disenchantment there developed what Taylor describes as the "buffered self," a new form of interiorized subjectivity that held an instrumental posture towards the world. Taylor writes:

> These represent profound changes in our practical self-understanding, how we fit into our world (as buffered, disciplined, instrumental agents) and into society (as responsible individuals, constituting societies designed for mutual benefit). But they are all the more firmly entrenched in that they dovetail perfectly with the major theoretical transformation of Western modernity, viz., the rise of post-Galilean natural science. This finally yielded our familiar picture of the natural, "physical" universe as governed by exceptionless laws, which may reflect the wisdom and benevolence of the creator, but don't require in order to be understood—or (at least on the first level) explained—any reference to a good aimed at, whether in the form of a Platonic Idea, or of the Ideas in the mind of God.[10]

This new form of self-understanding was the direct result of an "immanent" religious paradigm that manifested itself in "natural law" and deism. This religious paradigm, at first, remained open to the divine, or the transcendent, as a foundation for the articulating the moral "good."[11] However,

---

10. Ibid., 542.

11. Ibid., 543–44. Taylor argues that while the "immanent order can thus slough off the transcendent . . . it doesn't necessarily do so. . . . For many, their highest sense of the

as this view developed, the transcendent view of the divine that characterized the premodern enchanted view of the world was seen as a threat to the developing modern social order. Taylor writes, "The sense of being menaced by fanaticism is one great source of the closure of immanence. In many cases we have an initial movement of anti-clericalism, which ends up turning into a rejection of Christianity, or later into atheism."[12] The end result is what Taylor refers to as the "excarnation" of Christianity, or the "transfer out of embodied 'enfleshed' forms of religious life, to those which are more 'in the head.' In this it follows in parallel with 'Enlightenment,' and modern unbelieving culture in general."[13] The end result of this shift is the development of a new social imaginary, "atheistic humanism," focused upon human flourishing, human rights, and equality as the highest form of good.[14]

An important consequence of this shift in social imaginary is that certain forms of religious belief, like traditional forms of Christianity, are less plausible. However, Taylor emphasizes that this did not lead to a complete rejection of religious belief; instead, it produced new forms and modes of religious expression.[15] Taylor writes:

> The salient feature of Western societies is not so much a decline of religious faith and practice, though there has been lots of that . . . but rather a mutual fragilization of different religious positions, as well as the outlooks both of belief and unbelief. The whole culture experiences cross pressures, between the draw of narratives of closed immanence on one side, and the sense of their inadequacy on the other, strengthened by encounter with existing milieux of religious practice, or just by some intimations of the transcendent.[16]

While this new social imaginary has made certain forms of religious belief more problematic it did not lead to the elimination of religion. Instead, it has led to development of new forms of religious expression in the West

---

good has been developed in a profoundly religious context. . . . Their sense of the highest good . . . is of something consubstantial with God; by that I mean that this good is inconceivable without God, or some relation to the higher." Ibid.

12. Ibid., 546.
13. Ibid., 554.
14. Ibid., 569.
15. Ibid., 594.
16. Ibid., 595.

that exist alongside increasingly accepted forms of unbelief. A significant consequence of this shift in social imaginary has been the rise of religious uncertainty. Taylor writes, "As well as inspiring the creation of new positions, new ways of rejecting religion which avoid the repugnant consequence, these cross pressures can lead to a condition where many people hesitate for a long time in their attitude to religion."[17]

Here Taylor provides an important cultural understanding of the current problem of young people leaving Christian faith. While much of the literature in youth ministry frames the problem within the context of the practices of the Christian community, Taylor's arguments force the Christian community to ask deeper questions about the influence of contemporary social imaginary in which young people form identity. These arguments provide a philosophical and cultural context in which Smith's "Moralistic Therapeutic Deism," as a contemporary expression of religious belief, makes perfect sense. Taylor also demonstrates why the Christian community cannot expect to address this problem by focusing upon new, creative techniques for mediating Christian faith. Making young people learn the Nicene Creed, or convincing pastors to share the sermon through a video feed on Facebook, does not address the default paradigm, the social imaginary, by which young people construct identity and make sense of Christian faith.

This raises important questions regarding the effect of the current emphasis upon the cultivation of practices and processes to help Christian faith "stick." What if these processes end up contributing to the problem by implicitly affirming or reinforcing the modern social imaginary described by Charles Taylor? While these processes might address significant issues in the short term, it seems that such an emphasis could, in the long term, be counterproductive if they do not address the implicit paradigm by which young people interpret them. Just as important is the recognition that this modern social imaginary, while making much more space for unbelief, is itself grounded in a religious perspective. The rise of secularity can be traced through a transformation of religious experience, from the porous self to the buffered self, or from an external relation to the divine to an internal relation, one that leads to a society built upon the foundation of natural law and deism. While the trajectory of this shift undoubtedly leads to atheistic humanism and the rejection of belief, it is important to recognize how it is founded upon a specific religious perspective. In this way, to

---

17. Ibid., 598.

talk of young people "leaving faith" may not be the most appropriate way to refer to the current problem of young people departing from the church. Rather than leaving faith they are instead exchanging one form of faith for another, leaving behind certain forms of belief and practice that are difficult to sustain within the modern social imaginary, and taking on new forms of faith and practice that are much more compatible with the modern social imaginary. What is the nature of this "faith" to which they are turning? To explore this I turn to the rise of the disciplinary society and the thought of Michel Foucault.

Pastoral Power and the Disciplinary Society

In *Discipline and Punish* Michel Foucault provides an archeological account of modern disciplinary power. He differentiates between older forms of monarchal power that exerted control through physical punishment, torture, and death, and contemporary forms of modern power that focus on the organization of space and the regulation of movements within a panoptic system of observation. This new form of power establishes forms of discourse that produce truth and inscribe "normativity" within its subjects.[18] This means that modern institutions end up creating their own language and set of norms that eventually become part of what society considers to be true.

This new form of power is no longer dependent upon external punishment or force, but on the technical arrangement of space and discursive regimes of truth (a new set of norms) that together produce a subject. This new power is diffused within the social and cultural institutions of modernity (the school, hospital, military, and prison) as instruments that "supervises every instant" and "compares, differentiates, hierarchizes, homogenizes, excludes. In short, it normalizes."[19]

At the center of this new form of disciplinary power is what Foucault calls "pastoral power." Foucault argues that the development of ecclesiastical, or church, power and authority differed from the dominant form of political power in the ancient world. This new form of Christian power, according to Foucault, is, "salvation-oriented (as opposed to political power). It is oblative (as opposed to the principle of sovereignty); it is individualizing

---

18. Foucault, *Discipline and Punish*, 193.
19. Ibid., 183.

(as opposed to legal power); it is coextensive and continuous with life; it is linked with a production of truth—the truth of the individual himself."[20]

In the early development of Christianity the church developed techniques and practices that focused on the salvation of the individual for the "world to come." Along with external forms of discipline, this new pastoral power developed "internal" mechanisms like "confession" that observed the inner self and allowed inner secrets to be exposed.[21] In this way the church developed a form of power that could observe and discipline individuals by addressing not just the external person, but the inner person as well.

With the Reformation of the sixteenth and seventeenth centuries this form of pastoral power broke free from the church and was applied to the reform of society. Over time, the focus of this pastoral power shifted from an otherworldly form of salvation to an emphasis upon well-being and human flourishing in this world. Foucault describes how the word *salvation* took on a different meaning, particularly, "health, well-being (that is, sufficient wealth, standard of living), security, protection against accidents. A series of 'worldly' aims took the place of the religious aims of the traditional pastorate . . ."[22] This shift also led to the development of a new "priesthood" as leaders in business, politics, education, and medicine came to be seen as the authorities concerned with the well-being or "salvation" of society. This new form of power, according to Foucault, became a catalyst for the rise of the "disciplinary society": a cultural paradigm in which "an increasingly controlled, more rational, and economic process of adjustment has been sought between productive activities, communications networks, and the play of power relations."[23] This becomes the basis for a totalizing form of power that seeks to manage the possibilities of action open to the individual through technical organization (forms and rituals) and internal normalization (confession) as the individual is inscribed with a new discourse of truth.[24] Thus, the premise of this new form of pastoral power is the formation of an individual, not through coercion and force, but through a process of formation and internalization into a common regime of truth of the status quo.

---

20. Foucault, Rabinow, and Rose, *Essential Foucault*, 132.
21. Ibid.
22. Ibid.
23. Ibid., 137.
24. Ibid., 138.

—The Pastoral Power of the Modern Social Imaginary—

Faith and Secularity

Together, the works of Foucault and Taylor speak to the religious nature of modern secular society. While the modern social imaginary makes atheism much more plausible as it problematizes certain forms of religious belief and practice, it is important to recognize that the development of the modern social imaginary can be traced back to religious impulses. In his work *Sources of the Self: The Making of Modern Identity*, Taylor explores the relationship between the modern understanding of the self and an Augustinian epistemology. Taylor writes, "The Augustinian proof moves through the subject and through the undeniable foundations of this presence to himself. Descartes was not alone in embracing the Augustinian path at the beginning of the modern era. In a sense those two centuries, the sixteenth and seventeenth can be seen as an immense flowering of Augustinian spirituality across all confessional differences . . ."[25]

He goes on to describe how Augustine anticipated Descartes. He writes, "Descartes is in many ways profoundly Augustinian: the emphasis on radical reflexivity, the importance of the cognito, the central role of a proof of God's existence which starts from 'within.' From features of my own ideas, instead of starting from external being . . . all put him in the stream of a revived Augustinian piety which dominated the late Renaissance on both sides of the great confessional divide."[26]

As Taylor traces the development of the modern understanding of the self he follows a religious path from Augustine, through Descartes, through Locke and Rousseau: a path that is fundamentally grounded in Christianity. While he describes how it moves from an orthodox version of Christian belief into forms of Deism and pantheism, it is important to recognize that the rise of secularity, and the challenge to more orthodox forms of Christian faith, is itself grounded in religious, specifically Christian, belief. Taken together with Foucault's discussion of the new form of "pastoral power" unleashed into the broader social and cultural institutions of society, it is clear that whatever atheistic or antireligious characteristics the modern social imaginary may now represent, it developed out of social and cultural patterns made possible by religious belief.[27]

25. Taylor, *Sources of The Self*, 141.
26. Ibid., 141, 143.
27. For a discussion of the religious foundation of secularity, see Vattimo, *After Christianity*.

This has significant implications for the way in which the current problem of young people leaving the church is framed. If the issue is described as young people leaving or abandoning "faith" it comes off as if young people who embrace secularity are embracing an areligious or antireligious way of life. The phrase "leaving faith" makes it seem as if an abandonment of institutional or orthodox forms of Christianity is to decide for nonfaith. However, as Taylor and Foucault demonstrate, it can be argued that secularity is itself grounded in a paradigm of faith, complete with its own form of "pastoral power" and "salvation."[28] In this context the issue becomes less about the abandonment of faith by young people and more about an exchange of one form of faith for another. To put it differently, rather than abandoning faith young people are exchanging what they consider to be an outdated, ineffective form of belief and practice for one that is more in line with the modern social imaginary.

The Religious Nature of Capitalism

Taylor argues in *A Secular Age* that secularity is not the absence of religious belief, even though it makes certain forms of religious belief much more difficult; instead, the rise of the secular society makes possible new expressions of faith undergirded by new forms of religious practice. Taylor summarizes this by writing:

> Thus my own view of "secularization" ... is that there has certainly been a "decline" of religion. Religious belief now exists in a field of choices that include various forms of demurral and rejection; Christian faith exists in a field where there is also a wide range of other spiritual options. But the interesting story is not simply one of decline, but also of a new placement of the sacred or spiritual in relation to individual and social life. This new placement is now the occasion for recompositions of spiritual life in new forms, and for new ways of existing in and out of relation to God.[29]

One of the more pervasive belief systems to develop in modernity is capitalism. The rise of exclusive humanism, as a part of the modern social imaginary, brought a new emphasis to such ideals as human rights, the ownership of property, and mutual benefit.[30] The increased prominence of

---

28. Ibid.
29. Taylor, *Secular Age*, 437.
30. Ibid., 160. Taylor writes, "In the next three centuries, from Locke to our day,

the economic and political spheres of cultural life can be interpreted as an important part of the shift from a premodern social imaginary, with its emphasis on the supernatural, to a modern social imaginary and its immanent focus on human flourishing. The religious principle of providence, a view of instrumental reason as a tool for humanity to cultivate dominion over creation, and the Protestant "sanctification of the ordinary life" created the conditions in which the immanent forces of economics and politics became the primary forces for ordering and governing society.[31] Whereas in a premodern society religious faith (traditions, customs, rituals) provided the glue that held social communities together, within modernity this function was taken over by economics.[32]

Philip Goodchild, in *The Theology of Money*, argues that this social transformation would not have been possible without a further development: the power and authority of money. More specifically, the development of a specific form of money: debt. He writes:

> The third impulse is the invention of a new kind of money, one that is created as debt. A debt is an obligation, a commitment to economic activity, and a commitment to repay money. It is a promise, and money holds its value as long as this promise is trusted. . . . A market based on debt money is an immanent system of credits and liabilities, of debts and obligations, and it is capable of unlimited growth. It ensures participation and cohesion, with promises of wealth and threats of exclusion, through a system of social obligations. Debt takes over the role of religion in economic life.[33]

Goodchild contends that the authority of money as debt and obligation took over the religious function of the church and its penitential system that focused on sin, atonement, and salvation. In the shift to a modern social imaginary, money becomes the last transcendent, universal foundation

---

although the contract language may fall away, and be used only by a minority of theorists, the underlying idea of society as existing for the (mutual benefit) of individuals, and the defense of their rights, takes on more and more importance." Ibid.

31. Ibid., 179.

32. Ibid., 181. See also Goodchild, *Theology of Money*. Goodchild writes, "The great transformation of modernity, then, involves a change that is at once both religious and economic and should be conceived under both registers simultaneously. The effective basis for trust and authority that daily ensures material and economic cooperation is no longer local custom or authoritative religious prescription. Distribution has to be effected by its own immanent, independent, or self-regulating order—the market" Ibid., xiii.

33. Ibid., xiv.

for society, and the eschatological hope for salvation and human flourishing. Money has become the ultimate ideology undergirding the new social world of modernity. Goodchild writes, "It is in modern life, rather than religious life, where ideology is most fully instantiated. If modern economic life differs essentially from religious life, it does so not because it possesses a truer understanding of its conditions of existence or of practical efficacy. The essential difference lies in its lack of consciousness. There is no need to venerate or even consider money, the source of the modern age. There is merely a practical need to make money."[34]

Goodchild argues that money is fundamentally religious because it "establishes patterns for living," and "contains its own principles according to which time, attention, and devotion are allocated."[35] It takes over the liturgical time of the church, establishing its own liturgical time, governed by the clock, which is a means of control and discipline. Goodchild demonstrates how money and capitalism take on a vital theological function. He writes:

> Since the value of money is purely ideal construct, the religion of money has its own theology. Its principles are fourfold: money is the promise of value on which actual value may be advanced; money is the supreme value against which all other values may be measured; money is a speculative value whose intrinsic worth waits to be demonstrated; and money is a debt or social obligation that requires that social activity be continually reordered around increasing profit and the repayment of debt, while also continually expanding the debt and obligation. Economic globalization is the universalization of this religion through its drive for growth and power, its progressive colonization of all dimensions of life, and its commitment to growing debt. A theology of money is required to explain the distinctive nature of this spectral power in the modern world.[36]

Taylor's work describes the historical, philosophical, and religious conditions that have produced a form of secularity in which "human flourishing" is the ultimate end and purpose of human life. The rise of the modern social imaginary makes this form of "exclusive humanism" possible by rendering traditional forms of religious belief problematic. An important theme running through Taylor's work is that this new form of humanism is itself the

34. Ibid., x.
35. Ibid., 6.
36. Ibid., 14.

—The Pastoral Power of the Modern Social Imaginary—

product of prior religious commitments and transformations. He writes, "Exclusive humanism in a sense crept up on us through an intermediate form, Providential Deism; and both the Deism and humanism were made possible by earlier developments within orthodox Christianity."[37] This development of the modern social imaginary, along with Philip Goodchild's articulation of the "theology of money," provides an important context in which to interpret the current secular global technocapitalist paradigm of Western society as an alternative version of "faith." Given Goodchild's discussion of the ideological and religious function of money, it is clear that the current dilemma of young people leaving the more traditional versions of Christian faith should not be articulated as an abandonment of faith. Instead, this phenomenon should be interpreted as the exchange of one version of religious belief and practice, one that is perceived to be dated and irrelevant, for another that is perceived to be a more relevant form of faith.

Clearly, the transcendent, mythical, nature of the orthodox Christian articulation of God, the good, and the salvific hope of redemption through the death and resurrection of Jesus Christ no longer grabs hold of the imaginations of young people living in the West. If Taylor and Goodchild are correct, this can in part be attributed to the immanent, more tangible, version of the good and salvation offered by the technocapitalist paradigm. The notion of salvation as human flourishing, as economic well-being and the accumulation of wealth, or as the making and remaking of one's identity through progress, fits within the way young people imagine the world. This new version of salvation and religious belief makes better sense as it fits the "fact" of the modern situation much better than the orthodox language of sin, resurrection, and a transcendent God.

Taylor points to this religious nature of secularity in his argument against other narratives of secularity. While the modern social imaginary has become firmly established as the way in which most people in the West make sense of the world, this does not mean that religion has been totally rejected. In fact, Taylor describes well the current dilemma facing the Christian community in his descriptions of religious perspectives. He refers to "the falling off, or alienation, from the Church and from some aspects of orthodox Christianity" but utilizes the label, taken from the work of Grace Davie, of "Christian nominalism."[38] He summarizes this phenomenon by writing, "So it appears that the religious or spiritual identity of

37. Taylor, *Secular Age*, 19.
38. Ibid., 520.

masses of people still remains defined by religious forms from which they normally keep themselves at a good distance."[39] He goes on to utilize Davie's description of this experience as "vicarious religion." He writes, "What she is trying to capture here is the relationship of people to a church, from which they stand at a certain distance, but which they nevertheless in some sense cherish; which they want to be there, partly as a holder of ancestral memory, partly as a resource against some future need . . . or as a source of comfort and orientation in the face of some collective disaster."[40]

What Taylor captures is a snapshot of religious experience in a time when the orthodox forms of Christian belief and practice have difficulty being fully integrated into the modern social imaginary. The modern understanding of the buffered self, along with the dominance of the techno-capitalist ordering of society, make it much more difficult to fully adhere to orthodox versions of Christian belief. Either young people must live with the tension, rationalizing it some way, or they must choose between a form of Christian fundamentalism and the modern secular life.

One way to hold the tension is to embrace the distinction between being "spiritual but not religious." Taylor notes this at the end of his chapter in which he describes religious experience in the context of the modern social imaginary. He writes, "Being 'spiritual but not religious' . . . usually designates a spiritual life which retains some distance from the disciplines and authority of religious confessions. Of course, the distance here reflects a reaction to religious authority claims, and a wariness of confessional leadership."[41]

This situation is characterized by "a certain diffuse ecumenical sense . . . and even those who subsequently take on some confessional life, and thus becomes religious, retain something of this original freedom from sectarianism."[42] Taylor ends with a quote from Mikhail Epstein's work describing the religious situation in post-Soviet Russia in which he invokes a saying of Berdyaev, "Knowledge, morality, art, government, and the economy should become religious, but freely and from inside, not by compulsion from outside."[43]

---

39. Ibid., 521.
40. Ibid., 522.
41. Ibid., 535.
42. Ibid.
43. Ibid.

An example of the tension between this new spirituality and traditional Christian belief can be seen in a discussion on the Apostles' Creed that took place in an introductory biblical theology course I teach to first-year college students. As I engaged the class on the meaning of Christ's resurrection as the basis for our eschatological hope I asked them, "How many of you know the Apostles' Creed?" Almost every hand went up. After explaining the creed to those who did not know I asked, "Do you believe the part about the 'resurrection of the body'?" Most of the students nodded their heads in affirmation. "Great," I said. I proceeded to talk about the Christian hope of the resurrection of the dead, and "heaven" as an embodied existence of a transformed creation, when a student interrupted me. "What do you mean 'our resurrection'? When we die we go to heaven, which has nothing to do with our physical bodies or this world." When I asked for clarification I found out that when they affirmed a belief in the "resurrection of the body" they meant the body of Jesus. When I told them that this is not the traditional meaning of the creed, and that this line refers to a belief in the resurrection of the dead, they were confused and many refused to believe me. For these students the resurrection of Jesus Christ was not, as Paul refers to it, the "first fruits" of our resurrection, it was the assurance that when we die we will go to heaven and live eternally as spiritual beings.

While the majority of these students come from churches grounded in the Reformed tradition where the creed is recited every Sunday, clearly their interpretation of the creed had been shaped by a modern social imaginary in which the true meaning of resurrection and human life is found in a radically transcendent spiritualized reality that signifies the overcoming of the temporal finitude of creaturely life.

A New Social Reality: Technocapitalism

A characteristic of the "secular age," as Taylor describes it, is the dominance of the economic sphere over all other spheres through the development of capitalism. The social glue of Western civilization, which was once orthodox Christian belief and practice, has been replaced by the capitalist economic paradigm. To be more specific, it is the global fusion of capitalism and technology that profoundly shapes the lived experience of young people in the West: a phenomenon known as "global technocapitalism."

Luis Suarez-Villa defines technocapitalism as the dominant power of the economic sphere—manifested in corporate power—that colonizes and commodifies every part of human social existence.[44] This encroachment into every area of social life is for the purpose of creating commercial value, or surplus value, out of every social and cultural activity. The driving force of this process is what Suarez-Villa calls "experimentalism," in which the goal of all technological and scientific inquiry is profit and power that is then used to reorganize, reshape, and recreate social patterns and cultural institutions.[45] Suarez-Villa summarizes this new form of capitalism this way:

> Technocapitalism is defined . . . as a new form of capitalism that is heavily grounded on corporate power and its exploitation of technological creativity. Creativity, an intangible human quality, is the most precious resource of this new incarnation of capitalism. Corporate power and profit inevitably depend on the commodification of creativity through research regimes that must generate new inventions and innovations. These regimes and the corporate apparatus in which they are embedded are to technocapitalism what the factory system and its production regimes were to industrial capitalism. . . . The generation of technology in this new era of capitalism is therefore a social phenomenon that relies as much on technical functionality as on the co-option of cultural attributes.[46]

The "truth" that informs every action and procedure in this new economic world view is the production of "commercial value . . . over all other possibilities."[47] This commercial, or surplus, value is what drives the mediation and production of social and cultural reality through new processes and techniques.[48] These techniques and processes create and define reality, resulting in the "subordination of life, nature, and human values to the ethos of corporate experimentalism . . . as social, cultural, and institutional restraints are collapsed by the new order."[49]

Supporting this new form of capitalism is an increased emphasis on the accumulation and proliferation of technological knowledge and

44. Suarez-Villa, *Technocapitalism*, 2.
45. Ibid., 8–11.
46. Ibid., 4.
47. Ibid., 13.
48. Suarez-Villa writes, "In the emerging era of technocapitalism, however, corporate power and commercial gain are the drivers of experimental endeavors. . . . Extracting commercial value out of research is therefore acquiring a higher priority than solving any specific technological problem." Ibid., 27.
49. Ibid., 16.

techniques that displace the old industrial economic structures and identity labels (white collar, blue collar, etc.). These structures are replaced with networks governed by the accumulation of information mediated through new technological forms.[50] An essential part of this development is what Suarez-Villa refers to as the "massification of higher education," in which higher education becomes the platform for new forms of knowledge to be created and diffused throughout society, while also providing the technological infrastructure and social networks needed to develop new forms of technology.[51] This new technological knowledge becomes the building blocks for new forms of economic and social power as "this new version of capitalism colonizes aspects of life and work that were untouched by prior stages of capitalism."[52] All of this is directed toward the cultivation of surplus value as the highest good in order to accumulate wealth and bring about the transformation of social life.

The problem with this new form of capitalism is that it represents the pervasive encroachment of the economic sphere into every area of cultural life. Suarez-Villa warns, "The new corporatism spawned by this new version of capitalism may not spare any aspect of life, society or nature. As it demolishes old structures and colonizes new areas, the new corporatism leaves little space for dissent, and very limited tolerance for those who obstruct its quest for power and profit."[53]

More than this, however, is the power and influence this new form of capitalism has upon the ways individuals and communities form meaning and identity. The technological processes even provide the opportunity to "produce individuals with characteristics that are highly desirable to corporatism. The 'design' or 'engineering' of humans with greater potential for creativity and innovation would be of great interest in this regard."[54]

50. Fisher, "Classless Workplace." Fisher writes, "Further bureaucratization and technocratization of postindustrial society means that the defining social division is no longer based on property relations between those who own the means of production and those who do not, but 'the bureaucratic and authority relations between those who have powers of decision and those who have not, in all kinds of organizations, political, economic, and social' (Bell 1973 [*Coming of Post-Industrial Society*], 119). In effect, Bell sees the postindustrial society as a classless society, with the axis of social power stemming from mastering the dominant means of production—information technology (that is, on meritocracy), rather than ownership of those means." "Classess Workplace," 182.

51. Suarez-Villa, *Technocapitalism*, 21.

52. Ibid., 32.

53. Ibid., 164.

54. Ibid., 161.

All of this points to the formative power that global technocapitalism exerts over the lived experience of young people in the West. The institutions and processes that mediate the social and cultural reality establish the social imaginary by which young people construct meaning and identity. The religious function of the technocapitalist world view is demonstrated in the reification of surplus value as the highest good that directs all practices and techniques. This commercialization of social and cultural relationships represents the desire to transcend historical and material conditions in favor of an abstract, monetized reality through new forms of knowledge. As we will see in the next chapter, this same desire causes young people to anxiously construct and reconstruct a monetized, commodified identity that is both desirable and consumable within the networks of social and cultural power.

The pastoral, disciplinary function of contemporary institutions contributes to this by implementing techniques and processes that continually cultivate this desire in the form of knowledge, jobs, health, and sexuality. Through this experience young people are conditioned to desire this "surplus value"—the reification of ideal humanity—through processes that emphasize improvement, growth, perfection, and the transcendence of natural limitations. In all of this technocapitalism offers its own version of salvation, transcendence, and desire that condition young people to take their place within the technological and scientific networks that offer the greatest possibilities for employment, wealth, and well-being. The alternative, which will be discussed in the next chapter, is to be ejected from the networks of power as a failed commodity.

Conclusion: A New Form of Faith

Taylor's purpose in describing the rise of secularity and the dominance of the economic sphere is to help make sense of the changes to religious belief and practice within contemporary Western culture. The point is not to reclaim some earlier age of religious belief—the Protestant reforms of the sixteenth century, including the social and cultural changes they produced, have led to positive developments that need to be affirmed.[55] Secularity is itself a positive development that, it can be argued, is an outworking of a Pauline interpretation of Christianity.[56] The point, for Taylor, is not to

55. Taylor, *Secular Age*, 772.
56. See Vattimo, *After Christianity*.

turn back the clock, but to recognize the unintended consequences of these reforms: particularly, the warping of secularity into a form of "secularism" that is a "narrower, more homogeneous world of conformity," and a distortion of the Christian life.[57]

As discussed above, one way to name this "distortion of the Christian life" in the lives of young people is the prevalence of Moralistic Therapeutic Deism as indicated in the research of Christian Smith, and, as was described above, can be summarized by the following beliefs:

1. A God exists who created and orders the world and watches over human life on earth.
2. God wants people to be good, nice, and fair to each other, as taught in the Bible and by most world religions.
3. The central goal of life is to be happy and to feel good about oneself.
4. God does not need to be particularly involved in one's life except when God is needed to resolve a problem.
5. Good people go to heaven when they die.[58]

Together, the works of Suarez-Villa and Goodchild provide an important sociological and cultural context in which the religious focus of Moral Therapeutic Deism can be reinterpreted and redescribed in the following way:

1. A transcendent power (the market) creates and orders the world through technological patterns of production and consumption.
2. The market wants people to continuously improve in the interest of progress and the good of society.
3. The goal of life is to attain happiness by maximizing desirability and attaining the ideal life of wealth and influence.
4. The market provides the means for the continuous creation and recreation of identity that prevents a loss of desirability and network alienation.
5. The goal of life is to establish an identity that transcends human finitude and death.

---

57. Taylor, *Secular Age*, 772.

58. See the definition discussed above as given by Christian Smith in *Soul Searching*, 162.

This reinterpretation demonstrates the important relationship between Moral Therapeutic Deism and global technocapitalism as an articulation of the purpose and meaning of human life.

The problem with the current literature that addresses the issue of young people leaving the church is that it does not take seriously the influence of the modern social imaginary as the context for Moralistic Therapeutic Deism. As the social and cultural patterns of the West emphasize efficiency, effectiveness, and the cultivation of surplus value through new forms of technical and scientific knowledge, a "religious" focus upon morality, human flourishing, and an invisible "ruling hand" becomes much more likely. Many of the authors emphasize the influence of cultural changes upon the way young people form religious beliefs, even calling for new forms of practice to speak to these new conditions. However, they fail to adequately engage the deeper social imaginary that influences the way in which the Christian tradition is heard and understood. To focus upon the development of practices that make faith "stick," that place Jesus at the center, or that develop new, culturally relevant expressions of Christian belief, all fail to take into consideration the ways in which the global technocapitalist social imaginary shapes how young people make religious meaning and construct religious identity.

Just as important is the pervasive influence and effect the technocapitalist social imaginary has upon the lived experience of young people in the West. It is this experience we will explore in the next chapter.

Chapter 4

Failed Commodities

During their time on the Axiom, EVE and WALL-E are sent to the repair ward—the place where robots that no longer function the way they are supposed to go to get fixed. These are robots that no longer follow the lines, or operate within the range of what is considered normal and appropriate behavior. EVE is sent into a separate room for a cleaning and recalibration, while WALL-E is placed in confinement alongside the other malfunctioning robots. When WALL-E mistakenly believes that EVE is being tortured, he breaks out of his cell, crashes through the door, grabs EVE's arm, and accidently fires a laser shot that disables the entire ward, freeing all of the robots. In response, the motley crew of dysfunctional robots places WALL-E on their shoulders as a liberating hero. They roll through the ship, disregarding the lines and regulations as they confront security robots. Ultimately, this band of misfits plays an important role in helping WALL-E and EVE find the boot plant and return the Axiom to earth.

This comical scene raises important questions about the line that separates "normal" from "abnormal" and the how the threat of delinquency or abnormality plays an important role in maintaining the status quo. The social imaginary of the Axiom, with its structures, procedures, and lines not only employs a positive form of discipline focused on right behavior, but it at the same time imposes a negative form of discipline with the threat of being sent to the repair ward. The repair ward is not just a place where broken robots can get fixed, it is also a place where robots that refuse to cooperate, or somehow represent a threat to the order of the Axiom, are monitored and controlled. This is the case with WALL-E and EVE, who are sent there because the boot plant they carry poses a threat to AUTO and the life of the Axiom. All of this relates to Foucault's work in *Discipline and Punish* that speaks to the new techniques of discipline and control within the development of modern society. He argues that "the normal" is a powerful tool of coercion used to reinforce the truth of modern social life by establishing a set of standards that homogenize social life by differentiating what is acceptable from that which is different.[1] This coercive force embeds itself within the institutions and patterns of modern life as a "regime of truth"—a discourse that guarantees the survival of a particular way of life by establishing the norms for social life. Or, to put it in the negative, those individuals, practices, and beliefs that pose a threat to the status quo are labeled "abnormal" or "delinquent" as they are cut off from cultural power through incarceration, exile, or rehabilitation.

The disciplinary power of the Axiom uses the repair ward as a way to silence WALL-E and EVE and derail their mission. As we will see, this type of power is also part of the technocapitalist social imaginary that establishes its own regime of truth with its own version of what is "normal" and "abnormal." This establishes the conditions for a profound form of anxiety that grips young people as they negotiate the networks and power structures of global technocapitalism and try to meet expectations and avoid the embarrassing stigma of failure.

One of the courses that I teach is an introduction to college seminar that helps students develop a sense of calling and vocation by relating their field of study to the broader theme of God's work in the world. An assignment I regularly give is to have students write a short paper naming their greatest fears and anxieties as they begin their college career. Recently, when I asked for a volunteer to share with the rest of the class, a young woman talked about her greatest fear: failure. With tears in her eyes she talked about her fear that she would never live up to the expectations of the adults in her life. When I asked about her family she indicated that they were very close and that she loved them very much. However, she went on to talk about the pressure she feels to perform, even providing a list of the areas of life in which she feels it the most: academics, athletics, employment, and religion. She talked about the anxiety that is driven by a desire to be successful at everything, including her church life, and she ended her comments by describing the anxiety she felt about college and finding a good job.

---

1. Foucault, *Discipline and Punish*, 184.

—Failed Commodities—

When she finished speaking I asked the class if there were others who shared the same fear and anxiety about performance and success. Every one of the sixteen students in the class raised their hands. For the remainder of the hour I listened as students shared their fear and anxiety about not measuring up, about not being successful, and about disappointing the adults in their lives. One student shared that he would rather not try, he would rather not attempt a task or assignment, than take the risk, put forth effort, and fail. These students' identity was wrapped up in their ability to perform well and their ability to become successful in the broader social and cultural world.

Any attempt to address the issue of young people leaving the church has to seriously examine how the social and cultural patterns of global technocapitalism attempt to manage the lives of young people. While it is important to recognize the diversity that exists among young people, it is just as important to acknowledge the homogenizing effect of the technocapitalist paradigm as it flattens cultural space. An important part of this is the way the names and values of Western culture are inscribed into the identity of young people. This produces the anxiety and fear described above as young people live into these cultural expectations. It is this experience that shapes the social imaginary of young people in the West as it opens and closes the possible ways they encounter the world.

The purpose of this chapter is to explore how the modern social imaginary is inscribed into the identity of young people by the social and economic structures of global technocapitalism. Given Taylor's account of the development of the secular society and dominance of the economic sphere of cultural life, it is important to explore how this affects the way young people make meaning of the world and how they understand issues of identity and religious belief. As capitalism shifts into a new postindustrial, knowledge-based form of technocapitalism, one way to frame this transformation is in the terms of a move from a "society of production" to a "society of consumption."[2] It is this consumerist transformation that has profoundly shaped the way young people make sense of their identity and religious experience. The question for the Christian community is this: What are the effects of this new reality upon the way young people construct identity and meaning? Furthermore, how have these conditions

---

2. Zygmunt Bauman uses this terminology to discuss the economic shift that has taken place within capitalism in the West. See *Consuming Life*.

influenced the way young people understand the meaning and purpose of religious belief and practice?

Young People and the Consumer Society

Zygmunt Bauman, in his book *Globalization: The Human Consequences*, describes the phenomenon of globalization as the technological compression of time and space that places a high value on change and mobility. This establishes a cultural condition in which there are increasingly no longer boundaries. People are constantly on the move, constantly in a state of transformation, and constantly transversing limits—cultivating a form of desire for which there is no satisfaction. All of this establishes the conditions for the creation of a "consumer society."[3]

It is this emphasis on technology and change that helps to explain the shift in the West from a "society of producers" to a "society of consumers." The previous mode of industrial capitalism focused on production as the way to attain long-term security, as communities met their needs through the production of durable goods and the collective attempt to establish regular patterns of behavior and modes of production. At the center of this society was capital: raw materials, the development of factory systems, and the institutions and cultural patterns that both mediated and guaranteed this way of life. With the onset of globalization and the new economy this way of life began to drastically change. While a "society of producers" focused on attaining stability by meeting the basic needs of life, a "society of consumers" focuses on meeting the "rising volume and intensity of desires," which rapidly increases the cycle of production and consumption. Bauman writes, "New needs need new commodities; new commodities need new needs and desires; the advent of consumerism augurs the era of 'inbuilt obsolescence' of goods offered on the market and signals a spectacular rise in the waste disposal industry . . ."[4]

In order to be a prominent member of this new "society of consumers" individuals must constantly make and remake their identity. Given the emphasis on innovation through the cultivation of new forms of knowledge, and given the rapid speed at which technology enables the destruction and recreation of commodities, the new social reality for individuals is that they

---

3. Bauman, *Globalization*, 79.
4. Bauman, *Consuming Life*, 31.

must at the same time become both consumer and commodity.[5] To put it simply, individuals must become a consumable product that others desire. Bauman writes:

> To enter the society of consumers and be issued permanent residence permits, men and women must meet the conditions of eligibility defined by market standards. They are expected to make themselves available on the market and to seek, in competition with the rest of the members, their most favorable 'market value.' While exploring the marketplace in search of consumer goods . . . they are drawn to the shops by the prospect of finding the tools and raw materials they may (and must) use in making themselves 'fit for being consumed'—and so market worthy.[6]

The drive for security within this new social paradigm manifests itself as the drive to be desired, to be "ahead of the style pack," which holds the "promise of a high market value and a profusion of demand (both translated as a certainty of recognition, approval and inclusion)."[7] Ironically, these new social conditions mean that security is elusive if not impossible because of the need to keep up with the rapid pace of change. Individuals must constantly make and remake their identity in order to ensure their continued status and participation in the consumer society. This creates a situation in which a person's status within social and cultural networks is largely dependent upon the individual's ability to commodify his or her identity in a way that is desirable to others.

The consequence of this new social and cultural situation, for Bauman, is a Promethean making and remaking of the world through new processes and techniques for the purpose of perfecting human existence and improving the world. It is a situation in which "the shape of the world—its degree of perfection" becomes a "matter of human concern and human purposeful action."[8] Whereas in the "society of production" this task was seen as a collective responsibility, the shift to the consumer society, with its emphasis upon individuation and commodification, leads to an emphasis on the individual "as simultaneously the main object and the main subject of the

---

5. Ibid., 12. Bauman writes, "In the society of consumers no one can become a subject without first turning into a commodity, and no one can keep his or her subjectness secure without perpetually resuscitating, resurrecting and replenishing the capacities expected and required of a sellable commodity." Ibid.

6. Ibid., 62.

7. Ibid., 83.

8. Ibid., 58.

duty to remake the world, as well as of the responsibility for its fulfillment or failure . . ."⁹ As the "society of consumers" constantly develop new and better products through new and more efficient forms of technology, there also develops a form of "Promethean shame," which Bauman describes this way:

> Promethean shame is a sentiment which "overwhelms men and women at the sight of the humiliatingly high quality of things they themselves fabricated". . . . The "raw" unadorned, unreformed and unprocessed body is something to be ashamed of: offensive to the eye, always leaving much to be desired, and above all a living testimony to a failure of duty, and perhaps to the ineptitude, ignorance, impotence and resourcelessness of "the self." The "naked body," the object which by common consent should not be publicly exposed for reasons of the decorum and dignity of its "owner," these days does not mean, Anders suggests, "the body unclothed, but a body in which no work has been done"—an insufficiently "reified" body.¹⁰

Within the social imaginary of the "society of consumers" the natural limitations that are a part of being human—finitude, vulnerability, and suffering—are resented; they are loathed and feared as "illegitimate and thus unacceptable constraints imposed upon the individual liberty to choose."¹¹ Thus, human nature must be overcome through the accumulation of new knowledge, new techniques, and new commodities. This vision of human improvement and transcendence is the salvific drive of technocapitalism that holds out the promise of an idealized, fabricated identity that is forever desired and consumed.

This new social existence can be framed in the religious language of transformation and sanctification in which individuals are constantly making and remaking their identity to become members of the consumer society. This lifelong performance is fueled by the anxiety and fear of being rejected as a "failed consumer," which means being relegated to the fate of useless waste—to become nothing.¹²

9. Ibid.
10. Ibid., 59–60.
11. Ibid., 114.
12. Ibid., 64–65. Bauman writes, "A considerable number of consumers de jure fail the test which has been set, informally yet all too tangibly, for consumers de facto. Those who fail the test are 'failed consumers,' sometimes subcategorized as 'failed asylum seekers' or 'unlawful immigrants,' at other times as the 'underclass' (that is, a motley assortment of

—Failed Commodities—

Henry Giroux, in his book *Youth in a Suspect Society: Democracy or Disposability*, uses Bauman's description of identity within the consumer society to describe how young people are being commodified through the economic and social processes of technocapitalism.[13] Increasingly, educational institutions at every level are being reappropriated for the purposes of global technocapitalism. As the economy shifts from material-based production to information or knowledge-based production, education has become deeply embedded within the economic processes of the West. Increasingly, Giroux argues, education is commodified as it comes under the influence of economic and ideological forces that "narrow its legitimacy and purview" from what is often referred to as a liberal education to a more technical approach.[14] All of this is taking place as new forms of "biopolitical" are being formed that attempt to "regularize" and "produce" new ways of being in the world.[15] Giroux writes, "Populations are now controlled not simply through the threat of force but through technologies of consent produced in a vast array of apparatuses extending from the school to the varied instances of screen and electronically mediated culture. Central to the new form of neoliberal biopolitics is the issue of how youth are to be defined, guided, constituted, governed, and at times abandoned in accordance with a market based rationality and logic of accumulation."[16]

As the lives of young people become increasingly commodified as a part of the consumer society, they are being inscribed with a particular social imaginary, or way of being in the world, that is attuned to the impulses of the market. Whereas former manifestations of modernity used forms of supervision and discipline to form and shape identity, young people living in the new consumer society discipline themselves as they appropriate the tools and techniques necessary to become successful members of the

---

individuals refused access to any of the acknowledged social classes, ineligible for class membership as such), but most of the time scattered anonymously in the statistics of the 'poor' or 'people below the poverty line'—according to Simmel's classic definition the objects of charity, rather than discerning/choosing subjects like the rest of the members of the society of consumers. . . . It is there, at the meeting place of sellers and buyers, that selecting and setting apart the damned from the saved, insiders from outsiders, the included from the excluded (or, more to the point, right-and-proper consumers from flawed ones) is daily performed." Ibid.

13. See also Barber, *Consumed*.
14. Giroux, *Youth in a Suspect Society*, 114.
15. Ibid., 30.
16. Ibid.

consumer society. Through the pedagogy of the market, and the institutions that legitimize the market, young people are inscribed with a desire to constantly reconstruct their identity, driven by fear, anxiety, and insecurity which they are left to deal with on their own. Giroux writes, "Within this discourse, young people are called upon to deal with their lack of self confidence, powerlessness, and the endless indignities heaped upon them in a consumer society by employing utterly privatized and individualized solutions to what are 'socially produced discomforts.' The result is that they can locate the source of their troubles only in themselves . . ."[17]

Should young people fail, or should they decide to opt out, they are labeled as problematic, or worse, they are criminalized. Giroux echoes Bauman in describing how young people who are labeled "failed consumers" become a form of human "waste" that is ejected from the networks of power and influence.[18] Giroux writes:

> They are the outlaws of the market, flawed as consumers and devalued as commodities, and they pose ethical and political problems for a neoliberal biopolitics that defines itself as the apogee of freedom and democracy. Unable to participate in the rituals of status-seeking consumption, those "othered" in a consumer society are subject to a "new lexicon of cultural domination and symbolic violence [that] distributes shame and humiliation to those lower down the hierarchy." They also bear "the pain of failure, of being a loser, of being invisible to those above".f . . . These new waste products of a consumer society include the poor, the jobless, immigrants, youth, and other individuals and groups who occupy a limited space marked by insecurity, uncertainty, and deprivation.[19]

They are, as both Giroux and Bauman emphasize, better off if they "disappear."[20]

This analysis is supported by the fear and anxiety expressed by young people. Many fear that they will not be able to remake themselves in a way that will be accepted. They fear that their performance will not measure up, and that this failure will result in something worse than death—insignificance. What Bauman and Giroux address are the new cultural realities

17. Ibid., 59.
18. Ibid., 38.
19. Ibid.
20. Ibid., 39.

unleashed by technocapitalism as the West is transformed from a "society of production" into a "society of consumption." What is more important are the profound implications of this transformation on the lived experiences of young people as these new social and institutional conditions change the way young people construct identity and make meaning of the world.

This new social and cultural situation also has an impact on the way young people experience Christian belief and practice. On the one hand, it influences the way the tradition is communicated to and received by young people, which undoubtedly contributes to the problem of young people disconnecting from the church and orthodox forms of Christian faith. However, what influences this reception is how this new social and economic reality is inscribed into the identity of young people, shaping their interpretation of the world, and drastically affecting the way they experience religion and think about "salvation," "transcendence," and "human flourishing."

The Religious Function of the Consumer Society

Bringing the social and cultural transformation of the consumer society into dialogue with Taylor and Foucault provides an important lens for interpreting the religious experience of young people living in the West. Taylor's exploration of the "secular age" describes how transcendence is collapsed into the "immanent frame" of atheistic humanism and human flourishing that represents a radical shift in social imaginary, from an emphasis on the supernatural to a world view focused upon the power to remake or construct the world through processes and techniques of scientific inquiry. Ultimately, for Taylor, this modern turn represents a radical transformation of sovereign power and transcendence that has created the conditions in which the economic and political spheres become dominant.

Michael Hardt and Antonio Negri describe this transformation of sovereign power as the rise of a new form of "empire," in which transcendence is collapsed into the immanent material conditions of economic life. They write, "In politics, as in metaphysics, the dominant theme was thus to eliminate the medieval form of transcendence, which only inhibits production and consumption, while maintaining transcendence's effects of domination in a form adequate to the modes of association and production of the new humanity. The center of the problem of modernity was thus demonstrated in political philosophy, and here was where the new form of mediation found its most adequate response to the revolutionary forms of immanence: a transcendent political apparatus."[21]

What is important to recognize is that transcendence does not disappear; it is transformed from one manifestation (the divine right of monarchy)to another (the human rights of democracy). The supernatural approach to power that supported monarchies during the medieval period does not just disappear—it is transformed into new forms of transcendence and abstraction that guarantee the modern social imaginary and the dominance of the economic sphere. Thus, the form of empire that develops from this context is governed by the transcendent power of money reinforced by the ideology of global technocapitalism. Here we can make an important connection to the religious experiences of young people. Just as transcendence does not disappear, but is transformed into new, immanent expressions, so too the phenomenon of young people leaving the church must not be interpreted as the loss or absence of faith, but the transformation of "faith" from one religious expression (Christianity) to another (global technocapitalism).

An essential part of this new mode of sovereign power and transcendence is the "pastoral power" that knows the "inside of people's minds," in order to direct the individual conscience.[22] Foucault writes, "This form of power that applies itself to immediate everyday life categorizes the individual, marks him by his own individuality, attaches him to his own identity, imposes a law of truth on him that he must recognize and others have to recognize in him. It is a form of power that makes individuals subjects."[23]

No longer is this pastoral power directed toward some eternal supernatural world; instead, "salvation" is understood to be about human flourishing as it addresses the immanent, material conditions in which people live. Within the paradigm of global technocapitalism this pastoral power is directed towards a reified, commodified self that maintains desirability through the practice of continuous consumption. The formative power of technocapitalism inscribes itself within the subject through the "free" act of consumption, bringing transcendence from the realm of the supernatural into the immanent economic experience of the individual in the form of a reified identity that provides the catalyst for an endless cycle of commodification and consumption.

21. Hardt and Negri, *Empire*, 83.
22. Foucault, Rabinow, and Rose, *Essential Foucault*, 132.
23. Ibid., 130.

—Failed Commodities—

This religious function of technocapitalism and the consumer society can be found in Adam Smith's description of the "invisible hand" that miraculously transforms self-interest into a benefit for the greater society, a claim that embeds the transcendent firmly within the realm of economic relations as a way to cultivate and ensure the "well-being of individuals."[24] Hardt and Negri write:

> The political transcendental of the modern state is defined as an economic transcendental. Smith's theory of value was the soul and substance of the concept of the modern sovereign state.... Modern European sovereignty is capitalist sovereignty, a form of command that over-determines the relationship between individuality and universality as a function of the development of capital.... When the synthesis of sovereignty and capital is fully accomplished and the transcendence of power is completely transformed into a transcendental exercise of authority, then sovereignty becomes a political machine that rules across the entire society.[25]

The "redemptive" vision of technocapitalism and the consumer society can be articulated as a form of personal salvation from the void—the chaotic nothingness, or nonexistence, of the "failed consumer"—through a continuous cycle of consumption, commodification, and identity construction.[26] Bauman uses explicitly religious language to describe this process by referring to it as the constant struggle to be "born again"—continually cutting ties with the past in order to become something or someone else.[27] Sheldon Wolin, in his book *Democracy Incorporated: Managed Democracy and the Specter of Inverted Totalitarianism*, makes a similar claim about the contemporary secular society. He writes:

> Equally important, the culture produced by modern advertising, which seems at first glance to be resolutely secular and materialistic, the antithesis of religious and especially of evangelical teachings, actually reinforces that dynamic. Almost every product promises to change your life: it will make you more beautiful, cleaner, more sexually alluring, and more successful. Born again as it were. The messages contain promises about the future.... The virtual reality of the advertiser and the 'good news' of the evangelist complement each other.... Their zeal to transcend the

24. Hardt and Negri, *Empire*, 86.
25. Ibid., 86–87.
26. Bauman, *Consuming Life*, 160.
27. Ibid., 100.

ordinary and their bottomless optimism both feed the hubris of Superpower . . .[28]

From these examples it is clear that the social imaginary framing the lived experience of young people in the West is the modern rise of secularity and the transformation of sovereign power from the transcendent world of the divine to the "immanent frame" of economic capitalism. Therefore, the current issue of young people leaving the church and abandoning orthodox forms of Christian belief must be interpreted within the context of this lived experience. Rather than seeing the development of secularity and the dominance of technocapitalism as a rejection of religious belief and experience, it is important to recognize how this shift, and the social imaginary that it cultivates, is the result of a profound transformation of religious belief. The rise of empire and the consumer society represent a new form of sovereign power, desire, and salvation that is no less religious than the world of the 1500s. It merely represents a different form of religious belief and experience, one that is focused upon a "this-worldly" salvation as human flourishing and well-being, mediated through the transcendent power of money and markets.

Framing the issue this way allows the Christian community to broaden the scope of the dilemma. At issue is not just the failure of the church, parents, or institutions to pass on faith to their children; it is not just about practices of faith formation and discipleship. A crucial part of this issue are the new social and cultural patterns and the way in which these patterns inscribe a modern social imaginary within the subjectivity of individuals through the religious and pastoral function of the consumer society.

A way to name this new religious and cultural reality young people inhabit is with the term *Moral Therapeutic Deism*. Christian Smith's research into the lives of adolescents and "emergent adulthood," from which this term comes, addresses the constant state of social and cultural flux in which young people desperately construct and reconstruct identity. In chapter two of *Lost in Transition*, "Captive to Consumerism," Smith describes the variety of responses emergent adults provided to questions concerning consumerism and visions of the good life. His conclusions support much of what has been previously discussed concerning the pervasive influence of the consumer society upon the lives of young adults. He writes, "Soon we were nearly pushing the emerging adults we interviewed to consider any plausible problematic side to mass consumerism, if they could. They could

28. Wolin, *Democracy Incorporated*, 11–12.

not. Even when we started deliberately leading emerging adults to address such questions, very few wanted to go there. Most emerging adults simply had very little to say that was critical, nor were they worried or even much aware of the possible questions or concerns about mass consumerism. For the vast majority, mass consumerism was good, end of story."[29]

Smith supports this claim with the statistic that 61 percent of the emergent adults interviewed for this study had no reservations about the rise of consumerism. Thirty percent did have some concerns, but did not believe it was possible to change the consumerist reality. Ultimately, when it came to defining the good life, Smith writes, "Being materially comfortable is a key element in most emerging adults' life goals."[30] He concludes by saying that "Nearly all focus on a certain version of the standard middle or upper middle class dream that is centered not only on family but also on financial security and material comfort and consumption."[31]

Smith's research also confirms the notion that institutions of higher education are increasingly under the influence of the technocapitalist paradigm as they focus upon the production of new knowledge and the development of new forms of work. Smith writes:

> Most, though not all, emerging adults believe in the importance of finishing high school and getting a college education. Large numbers want to do well in school, go to college, get a degree, and put it to good use. But for most, the reasons they value college seem to have little to do with the broadly humanistic vision of higher education described above. Rather, their motivations have almost entirely to do with the instrumental advantages it produces for them as competitive individuals. . . . What really matters to emerging adults is getting the credits, earning the diploma, and becoming certified as a college-educated person so that they can get a better job, earn more money, and become a good salary earner and supporter of a materially comfortable and secure life.[32]

Smith's work provides an important sociological snapshot that supports the arguments of Bauman and Giroux regarding the impact of the rapidly changing social and cultural paradigm. His work also demonstrates the problem with responses that focus primarily on developing new processes

---

29. Smith et al., *Lost In Transition*, 72.
30. Ibid., 96.
31. Ibid., 100.
32. Ibid., 102.

and practices. They are problematic because these processes are often left disconnected from a thick description of faith and discipleship that connect them to the revelation of God and humanity in the crucified and risen Christ, leaving them susceptible to being co-opted by the pastoral function embedded within the techniques and processes of the consumer society.

What does this co-optation look like? It is the appropriation of techniques, practices, and processes that aim to transcend concrete human experience for an ideal, "spiritualized" human identity. Some exist primarily for the sake of meeting the expectations of adults in the Christian community who are anxious and afraid because the faith of young people does not look like their version of faith. Youth ministry, in this context, becomes a form of crisis ministry, sounding the alarm that young people are leaving the church while coming up with all sorts of practices, techniques, and strategies to address it.

Eventually this approach leads to the objectification of faith and the gospel as these strategies, practices, and processes become the primary focus. The unintended consequence is the establishment of a cycle of desirability in which young people perpetually try to meet, or in some cases purposefully not meet, the expectations of the adults in the Christian community. Through practices of piety, morality, and doctrinal beliefs, young people construct an identity that is desirable, or consumable, for the adults in the Christian community. They play the game, meeting expectations, living into the religious life as part of their construction of an ideal identity. Although these strategies and practices are intended to promote genuine Christian faith, if they remain disconnected from a thick description of faith and discipleship, they run the risk of being co-opted by the technocapitalist paradigm.

This is where the religious function of the consumer society and global technocapitalism and the practices and beliefs of the Christian community begin to intertwine. The Christian emphasis on a spiritualized and eternal heaven can make it seem as if this creaturely, material life is something to be overcome. While faithful living in this world is still seen as important, by framing salvation in the terms of a spiritual, otherworldly existence, human identity becomes an ideal, and at this point unattainable, vision of what it means to be human. Inevitably, the practices and processes of the Christian pastorally guide individuals toward this abstract human identity.

As has been demonstrated, the global technocapitalist consumer society provides its own vision of the ideal humanity framed in the language of money and human flourishing. Similarly, this vision of human life sees the material, creaturely existence as something to be overcome through technological processes and techniques. While the vertical transcendence of the supernatural has been replaced by an immanent transcendence of economic processes, there remains a transcendent universal that directs all things: the surplus value of money.

As young people inhabit the global technocapitalist world, and as they become inscribed with the social imaginary of the consumer society, these two forms of religious belief become conflated and interchangeable, until finally many young people exchange what they consider to be the outdated forms and language of Christianity for Moral Therapeutic Deism and the gospel of the consumer society.

What Should Be Done?

A proper response to the issue of young people leaving the church must be informed by an engagement of the social and cultural experience of young people in the West. This is more than changing the form of Christian practice in order to make the church more culturally relevant; it must also provide a critique of the current technocapitalist paradigm. By recognizing the religious nature of the technocapitalist paradigm the Christian community can become aware of how the institutional and cultural life of contemporary Western society forms the identity of young people. This interpretation of social and cultural praxis helps clarify the issue as young people exchanging one form of faith and praxis (Christianity) for another (technocapitalism).

Just as important, however, is a thick description of Christian faith that informs the practices of discipleship and faith formation. A problem with the current literature is that it takes faith for granted, assuming people know what it means to "trust" or "believe" in Jesus, leaving the processes of faith formation and discipleship vulnerable to co-optation by the dominant global technocapitalist ideology. In response, the Christian community should explore a weak theological response to the issue of faith and discipleship centered on Paul's proclamation of the crucified Christ. How does the crucifixion and resurrection of Christ short-circuit the religious function of the consumer society—Moral Therapeutic Deism? How does faith in the crucified and risen Christ affirm the goodness of finite, temporal life in this world? In other words, how does a weak theological approach interpret the gospel as a counternarrative to global technocapitalism?

To address these questions I will explore the theology of Dietrich Bonhoeffer, who provides a christological critique of an idealized humanity as well as a critique of an idealized, otherworldly interpretation of Christian faith. Bonhoeffer provides an articulation of the object of Christian faith, as well as the nature and purpose of the Christian church, that functions as an important foundation for the church to develop a counternarrative to the technocapitalist ideology.

CHAPTER 5

The Religious Problem

WALL-E DOESN'T BELONG ON the Axiom; clearly, he's an outsider. He's dirty, he doesn't follow the lines, and he is always surprised at how things function. It is also clear that WALL-E belongs "down below" in two ways: he's at home working in the garbage—the refuse and waste—and he was made to live and work on the earth. While the humans are obsessed with getting off the earth, WALL-E is drawn to it. In one scene, WALL-E clings to the side of a spaceship as it returns to the Axiom, and he looks back toward earth. Even though it is trashed, and satellites clutter the space around it, he is moved by its beauty. In the same scene WALL-E taps on the window, trying to help EVE see the beauty of the Milky Way and the rings of Saturn. Even though he is a robot, WALL-E is captivated by the material makeup of the universe.

This is why the label that he is given by MO (Microbe Obliterator) as he tries to clean him again and again is significant: WALL-E is a "foreign contaminant" to the life of the Axiom. He is a disruption, a rupture, a monstrosity. WALL-E's presence on the Axiom constantly disrupts the efficient processes that support the utopian life on the ship. He is a monstrosity in the sense that the humans and Axiom robots don't have the proper categories to make sense of him or integrate him into their structures and systems. In the end, WALL-E becomes the wrench in the gears of AUTO's attempt to preserve and maintain life on the Axiom.

More importantly, WALL-E functions as a sign and promise to the humans on the ship about what it means to live as a human being. WALL-E's humanity, grounded in his relational and cultural consciousness, sparks the humanity of others. John, who WALL-E helps back up into his chair; Mary, who WALL-E awakens from a screen-induced coma; and the captain of the ship, all begin to rediscover their humanity through encounters they have with WALL-E. They rediscover their creaturely existence: John and Mary splash around in the pool, and the captain spends time researching the memory of earth and the human activities of dancing and farming.

It is WALL-E's identity as a foreign contaminant that is the catalyst for the humans to leave the abstract world of the Axiom and return to earth. The driving force for this return is WALL-E's love for EVE, and her reciprocation of that love. WALL-E's presence injects love and realtionality into the sterile and individualistic world of the Axiom, where humans and robots are all self-sufficient as they float around on chairs and talk into screens. Everything he does flows out of his desire, his love, for EVE. It is this self-giving, sacrificial love that eventually pries open both robots and humans so they can see past their own directives, past their own utopian fantasies, to encounter others and finally embrace a creaturely life on earth.

Like the Axiom, the consumer society that young people inhabit abstracts and individualizes. Everything is about desirability, keeping one's place within the networks of power and influence. In many ways it is a world in which young people are more connected than ever, but they are still very much alone. In this situation the tendency of the church is to proclaim a strong theology complete with practices and processes to help build faith and build disciples. As we have seen, the problem with this approach is that it becomes one more cultural voice seeking to control, one more set of expectations that young people try to meet to be desired and keep their place within the network of the church.

A better response to this situation is one that is grounded in a weak theology. This is a theology that proclaims the revelation of the love of God for humanity in the crucified Christ—a love that pries humanity open, freeing us from every cultural power that abstracts and names, so we might live as human being in this world, embracing our finitude, our limitations, and ultimately our suffering. This is what it means to suggest that the best response to young people leaving the church is to let them go. Not to chase after them or hold on tightly, but to become open to them with a love that embraces their humanity, regardless of the choices they make. This is a love that invites young people to let go of the ideals and abstractions of the consumer society and embrace their own humanity, their own finite existence with all of its joy and suffering. We do this precisely because of God's love for humanity revealed in the crucified and risen Christ—a love that pries us open, frees us from every power at work in this world, and opens us up to encounter each other in love and grace. To unpack this interpretation of gospel I will explore the significance of weak theology in relation to the philosophical and theological work of Slavoj Žižek and Dietrich Bonhoeffer.

Secularity and The Monstrosity of Christ

One way to think about religion, or strong theology, is to see it as a way for individuals and communities to establish a sense of security. All cultural activity functions as a buffer. We create language and symbols to express our fears and project our fantasies; we narrate and renarrate the world in order to provide some sense of meaning and comfort. It is not enough to simply perform a task, to do something for its own sake, for every part of our existence begs for some higher or deeper meaning. We feel this overwhelming need to ground our actions in something above or beyond—something that helps us cope with the crushing monotony of the ordinary. So we rest in our fantasy, we weave our narratives and comfort ourselves with the belief that what we do and how we live matters. We justify our actions, our relationships, our lives, by higher principles that empower, console, inspire, and restrain. The result is a "normal" way of being in the world that follows the cultural expectation of a good and meaningful life.

Religion is an essential part of this cultural process. Humans have always appealed to some form of transcendence or the divine as a guarantee for reality. Whether it is struggling against the gods, wrestling with fate, or affirming providential love and care, the relationship between human life and divine transcendence has provided the catalyst for establishing, preserving, and transforming human culture. The way humanity thinks about itself and the world is bound up in religious thought and practice. This is not to say that religion is only a projection of human fantasy; it is, however, important to recognize the social and cultural function of religious belief.

Religion often functions like anxiety medication or a security blanket, soothing fear and guarding against despair. It provides a foundation for absolute forms of truth that become the guarantee for a particular world view or way of being in the world—metaphysical principles that order and govern the world. Liberal and conservative Christians, for example, can get caught up in trying to live according to principles that govern the way the Bible is read, and the way they live in the world, without inquiring as to whether these principles or ideals are actually grounded in the story of the death and resurrection of Christ. This results in the projection of an idealized heaven, some higher "good" or "truth" that ends up being a glorified version of our own fear and desire. As Taylor and Bauman's work shows, this fantasy has been transferred from religious beliefs and practices into the political, economic, and cultural patterns of the consumer society, in which we chase after an ideal life or some ideal identity that is always just out of reach, caught up in a desperate attempt to become something else or something more.

The consequence of this projected ideal life is that aspects of creaturely life are labeled as "abnormal," "delinquent," or "sinful." This is where religion provides the markers that distinguish what is normal and acceptable from that which is considered abnormal. At the same time religious language provides an excuse for inaction—for irresponsibility—for not getting involved in the muck and mire of lived reality. Holiness and transcendence become an excuse for hating and despising our neighbor, while mission and evangelism become a way to reform and remake the world in our own image. Empty clichés about "hating sin" while "loving the sinner" make it possible to not have to love anyone at all. The language of transcendence as some eternal otherness draws attention away from the reality that our feet are firmly planted on the ground. In the face of fear and anxiety, in the face of vulnerability and mortality, we are content, in the name of religion, to give up our humanity.

> Brothers and sisters, think of what you were when you were called. Not many of you were wise by human standards; not many were influential; not many were of noble birth. But God chose the foolish things of the world to shame the wise; God chose the weak things of the world to shame the strong. He chose the despised things—and the things that are not—to nullify the things that are, so that no one may boast before him. (1 Corinthians 1:26–29)

At the heart of the Christian message in Paul's letters is a call to love that weakens every form of cultural and religious ideology. In his letter to the Corinthians Paul testifies to the "weakness" or "foolishness" of the cross that stands in contrast to the strong Jewish religious expressions of the Jewish law and Greek cosmology. Throughout the letter Paul challenges the various forms of cultural power the Corinthian people use to justify their way of life as every cultural form of honor—including the hierarchical networks of brokered power—and shows how they are subverted by the cross of Jesus Christ. None of these cultural principles, for Paul, can provide the foundation for a way of life in the world. The only practice that is able to establish the conditions for human life existing in community is the way of love. Paul interprets the event of Christ's death and resurrection as the radical in-breaking of love that relativizes every totalizing truth and subverts every form of transcendence, opening the space for freedom and human subjectivity—making it possible for humans to live together in a community that takes difference seriously through the practice of grace.

This form of love grounded in the death and resurrection of Jesus Christ functions as a catalyst for secularization. The "death of God" on the cross is the revelation of the death of metaphysics and transcendence, the subversion of objectivity and absolute truth that gives way to subjectivity and interpretation. Nationality, race, gender, religion, economic status—these cultural constructions are no longer absolute, they no longer determine human identity. This is the subversive Christian core of secularity: that secularization is not the abandonment of Christianity; it is, instead, a continuation and development of the weakening rupture of the cross.

Philosopher Slavoj Žižek frames this interpretation of the death and resurrection of Christ in the language of "monstrosity." Monsters in literature and film signify an in-breaking of some alien presence that does not fit into neat categories. They are scary because they rupture the way people make sense of the world. They are frightening when they appear, but instantly we try to bring them under the control of language with new concepts that stitch the cultural tear back together, domesticating monsters in the name of stability, security, and peace.

Žižek interprets the crucified Christ as a monstrosity because of the way the cross disrupts our way of making sense of the world. Christian faith talks about the presence of God in this world by pointing to a broken, dying man suspended above the earth on an instrument of torture. It doesn't fit the cultural categories of God, the divine, or transcendence. After all, God is holy and all-powerful; God is transcendent and eternal. God doesn't suffer, God doesn't die, and God certainly is not vulnerable. In the place where divine transcendence and power is supposed to exist Christian faith declares weakness, darkness, and death. This, for Žižek, is monstrosity.

This interpretation emphasizes Christ's words from the cross: "My God, my God, Why have you forsaken me?" (Matt 27:46). This cry is more than just the complaint of a dying man, it is the ultimate negation of the transcendent Other as the metaphysical guarantee of reality. To make this point Žižek quotes G. K. Chesterton, who writes, "God is here no longer the miraculous exception that guarantees the normality of the universe, the unexplainable X who enables us to explain everything else; he is, on the contrary, himself overwhelmed by the overflowing miracle of his Creation."[1]

Žižek understands the death of Christ to be the radical rupture that sets humanity free from both the cosmological bondage of Greek metaphysics and from the radical transcendence of Jewish law. Here, Žižek aligns himself with Paul's interpretation of the cross as "foolishness to the Greeks and a stumbling block to the Jews" (1 Cor 1:23). The cross functions as a monstrous wrench in the gears of every form of cultural power. Every attempt to determine meaning and truth, for both Jews and Greeks, was based upon a radical, eternal transcendence untainted by the frailty and temporality of creaturely life. Cosmology and law were ancient forms of ideology that imposed and upheld social and cultural identity. The death and resurrection of Jesus Christ, for Paul, is the event that breaks open every ideal form of truth as it affirms human finitude and creaturely existence. In Jesus Christ God affirms not an ideal humanity, but a real humanity. In the death and resurrection of Jesus Christ God is at work creating a humanity that no longer finds its meaning in some eternal, ideal projection, but a humanity that lays claim to its vulnerable, inefficient, embodied life, which means that the cross is an "event" that stands over and against both the metaphysics of Greek cosmology and the legalism of Jewish law.

Žižek interprets Paul through the lens of Hegelian dialectic and Lacanian psychoanalysis in which the transcendent God is the forbidden Thing—the big Other—the law prevents humanity from attaining. Thus, the law perpetuates a desire for the forbidden thing with the false hope that if we obey fully one day we can have what we desire. This Lacanian emphasis focuses on the cyclical relationship between law and sin, as sin becomes a manifestation of the law—a continuous perpetuation of desire that keeps humanity in bondage. Within this interpretation of the law the crucifixion of Christ represents a violent rupture in the symbolic order by which the transcendent God is emptied—overcome on the cross—revealing that there is no radically transcendent Thing. Thus, on the cross the radically transcendent God dies—sacrificing God's self in order to free humanity from the cycle of law and sin, giving birth to the community of the Spirit that creates a radically new universal human subjectivity open to the possibility of a new life. Žižek writes, "What then is 'sublated' in the case of

1. Quoted in Žižek, Milbank, and Davis, *Monstrosity of Christ*, 88.

Christianity? It is not the finite reality which is sublated (negated—maintained—elevated) into a moment of ideal totality; it is, on the contrary, the divine Substance itself (God as a Thing in itself) which is sublated: negated (what dies on the Cross is the substantial figure of the transcendent God), but simultaneously maintained in the transubstantiated form of the Holy Spirit, the community of believers which exists only as the critical presupposition of the activity of finite individuals."[2]

In the crucifixion of Jesus Christ the transcendent, divine Other is emptied into the community of believers. This is a Trinitarian move as the Father sacrifices, or is "overcome," on the cross through the monstrosity of the Son, who in this mediation gives way to the emergence of Universal Spirit that is manifested in the particular community of believers.[3] The crucified Christ is a monstrosity because in him we discover "the appearance of God in the finite flesh of the human individual . . . a fragile, finite being as the revelation of God—a monstrous, grotesque "alien" that is the "more than human subject."[4] For Žižek, it is through the violent rupture of the cross and the vanishing mediation of the Son that humanity is set free for the radical subjectivity necessary for political action.

For Žižek, the death and resurrection of Jesus Christ provide powerful symbols and metaphors that challenge the ideology of global technocapitalism. In *The Fragile Absolute: Or Why is the Christian Legacy Worth Fighting For?*, Žižek brings the radical truth of Christianity into conversation with the problems associated with global capitalism where the present situation is one in which the dominant culture has become "less and less a specific sphere exempted from the market, and more and more . . . its central component."[5] For Žižek, the inherent violence of capitalism is seen in the homogenization of all cultural space by the market through the cultivation of desire and consumption.[6] The importance of Christianity—why he believes it is "worth fighting for"—is that the cross provides a powerful symbol of the dialectical rupture that is necessary for humanity to break out of the cycle of desire cultivated by global capitalism. Faith, in the Pauline sense, is a commitment to the universal truth of crucifixion that ruptures the ideology of liberal capitalism and opens the possibility for

2. Ibid., 61.
3. Ibid., 76.
4. Ibid.
5. Žižek, *Fragile Absolute*, 22.
6. Ibid., 12.

a radical politic grounded in love and charity. It is this love that becomes the basis for a universal justice, and for Žižek, a universal ethic that is not grounded in higher principles but what he refers to as a "cold and cruel passion."[7] He writes, "That is to say: what dies on the Cross is precisely the 'private' God, the God of our 'way of life,' the God who grounds a particular community. The underlying message of Christ's death is that a 'public' God can no longer be a living God: he has to die as a God. . . . Public space is by definition 'atheist.' The 'Holy Spirit' is thus a 'public' God, what remains of God in the public universal space: the radically desubstantialized virtual space of the collective of believers."[8]

Ultimately, Žižek sees the death and resurrection of Christ as the radical affirmation of this finite world. Over and against the strong power and totality of transcendence that is found in both religion and in capitalism, Žižek affirms the mystery revealed in Christian faith: that incompleteness is higher than completeness. For Žižek, the true achievement of Christianity is the elevation of a "loving imperfect Being to the place of God."[9] The consequence of this love is the possibility for a freedom that empowers humanity to embrace the monstrous finitude of this world.

Religionless Christianity

During his imprisonment by the Nazis Dietrich Bonhoeffer began to explore his own distrust of religion in letters written to his good friend Eberhard Bethge.[10] In a letter dated November 21, 1943, Bonhoeffer discusses his growing "suspicion and fear of religiosity."[11] He writes, "We are approaching a completely religionless age; people as they are now simply

---

7. Žižek, Milbank, and Davis, *Monstrosity of Christ*, 303.

8. Ibid., 295.

9. Žižek, *Fragile Absolute*, 139.

10. This engagement of Bonhoeffer's "religionless Christianity" follows Clifford Green's argument that these letters must be read in the context of Bonhoeffer's earlier work. Green writes, "Bonhoeffer's early theology must be understood as a 'theology of sociality.' Indeed, without diminishing later developments and new insights, the following argument shows that the concepts and concerns of his early theology continue to be formative for this whole thought." *Theology of Sociality*, 1. For alternative interpretations of Bonhoeffer's theology see the following: Dumas, *Dietrich Bonhoeffer*; Ott, *Reality and Faith*; and Phillips, *Christ for Us*. See also Zimmermann and Gregor, *Being Human, Becoming Human*, and Marsh, *Reclaiming Dietrich Bonhoeffer*.

11. Bonhoeffer et al., *Letters and Papers*, 362. Subsequently referred to as *DBWE* 8.

—THE RELIGIOUS PROBLEM—

cannot be religious anymore. Even those who honestly describe themselves as 'religious' aren't really practicing that at all; they presumably mean something quite different by 'religious.'"[12] He goes on to say, "How can Christ become the Lord of the religionless as well? Is there such a thing as a religionless Christian? . . . What does a church, a congregation, a sermon, a liturgy, a Christian life, mean in a religionless world? How do we talk about God—without religion . . . ?"[13]

Bonhoeffer came to the realization that every moral or religious principle that once provided European society with meaning had been drained away. A dramatic shift had occurred and religion was no longer the foundation for cultural life. Instead of trying to argue for Christianity, or give a defense of God, Bonhoeffer insisted that this new secular experience needed to be taken seriously. He criticized Christians who tried to retain a place for God by arguing against the new secular situation.[14] He writes, "I consider the attack by Christian apologetics on the world's coming of age as, first of all, pointless, second ignoble, and, third, unchristian. Pointless—because it appears to me like trying to put a person who has become an adult back into puberty, that is, to make people dependent on a lot of things on which they in fact no longer depend, to shove them into problems that in fact are no longer problems for them. Ignoble—because an attempt is being made here to exploit people's weaknesses for alien purposes to which they have not consented freely. Unchristian—because it confuses Christ with a particular stage of human religiousness . . ."[15]

At the same time, Bonhoeffer did not want to smuggle God into the secular world as a guarantee for piety or ethics; he was not interested in a God at the boundaries, a deus ex machina that provided answers for the problems that science, politics, and economics could not solve. Bonhoeffer wanted to take secularity seriously; he wanted to affirm Christ at the center of the secular society that had lost all sense of divine transcendence, meaning, and faith—for a world that had "come of age."

Bonhoeffer opposed religion because it rendered everyday life as secondary to a higher, spiritual reality. It was an oppressive means of control—a power play to justify one way of cultural life over all others. Religion turns God into a concept, the highest of ideals, that provides the foundation and

12. Ibid., 362.
13. Ibid., 363–64.
14. Ibid., 426–27.
15. Ibid., 427.

guarantee for meaning and morality, creating a radically transcendent god detached from human experience. Consequently, individuals and communities are caught up in a religious cycle of spiritual improvement, anxiously trying to attain an identity modeled after these higher principles and processes. Religion, in this context, is oppressive and dehumanizing as individuals frantically try to make and remake themselves in the image of an abstract projection of human identity.

Bonhoeffer addresses this issue by differentiating between "religion" and "faith" in the biblical stories of Adam and Jesus. "Religion" derives from the first Adam, who, by eating of the tree of the knowledge of good and evil in the garden of Eden, sought power and control over a world that was not his to control. "Faith" comes from the second Adam, Jesus Christ, who gave himself in love by dying on the cross. Religion is a power grab, taking hold of the world through violence and control; faith, by contrast, is grounded in the revelation or the givenness of the other. The first Adam sought control, the second brought love. One attempts to take the world captive, to remake god and neighbor into his own image and likeness, while the other opens himself up in love to the revelation of both God and neighbor.

Bonhoeffer, like Paul, maintains that truth can only be encountered in the weakening love of revelation; it is not found in the metaphysical truth of religion. In Jesus Christ the other is given as humanity is pried open to encounter God and neighbor. On the cross Jesus kills our selfish, inwardly curved humanity that tries to consume and control the world, he sacrifices the human propensity for metaphysical abstraction, and in Christ's resurrection humanity is opened back up to the possibility of love.

Religion and faith point us in different directions. Religion fosters an oppressive desire for ideal or "spiritual" principles that can never be attained, while faith opens humanity to encounter the other, directing humanity back to embrace this finite, temporal world. For Bonhoeffer, the revelation of God's love for the world in Jesus Christ means that humanity must no longer focus on some better, or higher, spiritual existence; instead, humanity is awakened to embrace this life. God is no longer the name for higher moral or doctrinal principles, God is revealed in the midst of the ethical encounter with the other. For Bonhoeffer, the death and resurrection of Jesus Christ awakens humanity to the demand of the "other"; it is this ethical demand that constitutes our human identity as we encounter and respond to the call placed upon us by our neighbor.

—The Religious Problem—

At the center of human identity, for Bonhoeffer, is love—a love for God and for our neighbor. Over and against the religious desire to violently dominate the other, faith cultivates a response of love that becomes the ground for freedom and grace. It is love that brings into existence a new form of community, the church, where the revelation of God's love for humanity is fully known.[16] This prompts Bonhoeffer to make what at first seems like a narrow religious claim that true knowledge of God, and therefore true knowledge of what it means to be human, is found only within the Christian community. He writes, "Community with God exists only through Christ, but Christ is present only in his church community, and therefore community with God exists only in the church."[17] However, what Bonhoeffer means is that the true revelation of God and human identity occurs in the concrete encounter of love revealed in the death and resurrection of Jesus Christ. This is what he means when he insists that Christ remain at the center of human social and cultural life—that true human identity is grounded in faith and love that opens us to encounter God as we responsibly embrace the world. The purpose of this community is not to close itself off from the world—it is not about putting up walls to keep people in—the purpose of this community is to exemplify this love in and for the world.

The pressing issue for Bonhoeffer was not trying to prevent the cultural shift to secularity, but figuring out what Jesus Christ means for those living in the secular age. The problem with religion is that it takes attention away from this world, and focuses it on some higher, spiritual reality. It cultivates an anxious desire that holds people captive to principles or ideals of spirituality and morality. Bonhoeffer's primary complaint against religious people is that they often appeal to these higher principles as justification for why they should not get involved in various issues; they evoke religion to evade their ethical responsibility. In "After Ten Years," Bonhoeffer writes:

---

16. Bonhoeffer, *Sanctorum Communio*, 166. Subsequently referred to as *DBWE* 1.

17. Ibid., 158. In the "Editor's Introduction" Clifford Green discusses the terminology Bonhoeffer uses to talk about the church. He writes, "*Gemeinde* is Bonhoeffer's preferred term; its meaning provides the theological norm for 'church.' When Bonhoeffer says, 'the church [*Kirche*] is Christ existing as *Gemeinde*,' this does not mean the institution calling itself the church defines where Christ is communally present. On the contrary, it is not a church organization that defines Christ, but Christ who defines the church. In other words, it is precisely where, and only where, 'Christ-exists-as-*Gemeinde*' that we find the 'church' (*Kirche*)." *DBWE* 1:14–15.

> In flight from public discussion and examination, this or that person may well attain the sanctuary of private virtuousness. But he must close his eyes and mouth to the injustice around him. He can remain undefiled by the consequences of responsible action only by deceiving himself. In everything he does, that which he fails to do will leave him no peace. He will either perish from the restlessness or turn into a hypocritical, self-righteous, small-minded human being. Who stands firm? Only the one whose ultimate standard is not his reason, his principles, conscience, freedom, or virtue; only the one who is prepared to sacrifice all of these when, in faith and in relationship to God alone, he is called to obedient and responsible action. . . .The ultimately responsible question is not how I extricate myself heroically from a situation but [how] a coming generation is to go on living. Only from such a historically responsible question will fruitful solutions arise, however humiliating they may be for the moment. In short, it is much easier to see a situation through on the basis of principles than in concrete responsibility.[18]

Christian faith, for Bonhoeffer, is an awakening—the death and resurrection of Jesus Christ frees humanity from abstract moral or spiritual principles so we can become responsible to this world. Ethical responsibility, in this context, is not about remaining clean; it is about courageously entering the fray, embracing this world and loving our neighbor by taking temporal life seriously. Christian faith is not about creating sectarian communities that protect and guard religious and moral principles; it is about fostering a way of being human in the midst of secularity that is grounded in grace and love.

Bonhoeffer's "religionless Christianity" stands in opposition to every social, political, and economic system that abstracts human identity and dehumanizes individuals and communities. Like Žižek's interpretation of the cross as monstrosity, Bonhoeffer's "religionless Christianity" provides a significant counternarrative to the lived experience of young people shaped by the social imaginary of global technocapitalism. For Bonhoeffer, the crucified and risen Christ subverts the human tendency for process and the reification of transcendence into ideal principles, focusing instead upon God's love for finite humanity. Bonhoeffer writes:

> Ecce homo—behold what a human being! In Christ the reconciliation of the world with God took place. The world will be overcome

---

18. *DBWE* 8:40, 42.

> not by destruction but by reconciliation. Not ideals or programs, not conscience, duty, responsibility, or virtue, but only the consummate love of God can meet and overcome reality. Again, this is accomplished not by a general idea of love, but by the love of God really lived in Jesus Christ. This love of God for the world does not withdraw from reality into noble souls detached from the world, but experiences and suffers the reality of the world at its worst. . . . Ecce homo—behold God become human, the unfathomable mystery of the love of God for the world. God loves human beings. God loves the world. Not an ideal human, but human beings as they are; not an ideal world, but the real world.[19]

For Bonhoeffer, the crucified Christ ruptures the closed circuit of religion and cultural ideology that draws the boundary lines determining what is desirable and normal, opening the space for a new form of human identity grounded in grace and love.[20] The technocapitalist processes that foster the desire to overcome or transcend humanity are short-circuited, freeing young people to embrace their creaturely finitude. As Bonhoeffer puts it, "[t]he form of the Crucified disarms all thinking aimed at success . . ."[21] Every form of commodification and objectification, every process or network that determines who is in and who is out, the successful from the human waste, is broken wide open by the cross. At the same time the resurrection of Christ undoes every attempt to appeal to an idealized eternity. Bonhoeffer writes:

> Where, however, it is recognized that the power of death has been broken, where the miracle of the resurrection and new life shines right into the world of death, there one demands no eternities from life. One takes from life what it offers, not all or nothing, but good things and bad, important things and unimportant, joy and pain. One doesn't cling anxiously to life, but neither does one throw it lightly away. One is content with measured time and does not attribute eternity to earthly things. One leaves to death the limited right that it still has. But one expects the new human being and the new world only from beyond death, from the power that has conquered death.[22]

---

19. *Ethics*, 82–83. Subsequently referred to as *DBWE 6*.
20. Ibid., 90.
21. Ibid.
22. *DBWE* 6:91.

In the crucified and risen Christ, Bonhoeffer discovers the affirmation of humanity living within the conditions of modern secularity. In the same way the cross negates every attempt to establish the absolute truth of religion, it also ruptures the cycle of desire and the abstraction of human identity perpetuated by the processes of technocapitalism. The good news for young people, according to Bonhoeffer, is that their real humanity is "the object neither of contempt nor of deification, but the object of the love of God."[23] The significance of this revelation of love, for Bonhoeffer, is that it is the affirmation of finite humanity.

At the same time, the resurrection of Jesus Christ opens the possibility for a new way of being in the world. Because the cross has freed humanity from religious and metaphysical principles, in the resurrection individuals and communities become responsible to live and act in response to the call of the other. This is a way of life marked by the courage to be for this world. Christian faith, for Bonhoeffer, means living at the center of cultural life. He writes:

> It always seems to me that we leave room for God only out of anxiety. I'd like to speak of God not at the boundaries but in the center, not in weakness but in strength, thus not in death and guilt but in human life and human goodness. When I reach my limits, it seems to me better not to say anything and leave what can't be solved unsolved. Belief in the resurrection is not the "solution" to the problem of death. God's "beyond" is not what is beyond our cognition! Epistemological transcendence has nothing to do with God's transcendence. God is the beyond in the midst of our lives. The church stands not at the point where human powers fail, at the boundaries, but in the center of the village.[24]

Christian love refuses to passively fall back upon the deus ex machine or appeal to moral principle as justification for not engaging the serious issues of this life. Instead, it calls for a form of "religionless Christianity" that takes up the responsibility to enter into the suffering of the other for the sake of the world.

This is the liberating message for young people who are caught in the dehumanizing processes of global technocapitalism. "Religionless Christianity" offers an interpretation of the death and resurrection of Jesus Christ that affirms secularity and the move of young people away from religious

---

23. Ibid., 93.
24. *DBWE* 8:366–67.

—The Religious Problem—

ideology. At the same time it challenges the new forms of religious ideology that exist within the economic and political processes of global technocapitalism. In the face of the anxiety and despair that young people experience as they frantically attempt to create and recreate a consumable identity, "religionless Christianity" invites them to a way of being that affirms their finite humanity. Rather than attempt to control or coerce young people to remain in religious institutions, or abandon them to the dehumanizing power of economic and political processes, the task of the Christian community is to enter their lived experience to help them embrace their finite humanity in a spirit of courage and love.

For Bonhoeffer, the absence of religious language or symbols that comes with secularity does not change the fact that the revelation of love in Jesus Christ is at the center of human life. Those who live within the social imaginary of secularity are either grounded in the revelation of faith and love (Jesus Christ) or they remain locked within an endless cycle of abstraction and reification in which human life is closed off from an encounter with the other (the being of Adam). Young people do not need one more set of religious processes; they need a community that responsibly calls them to embrace their humanity in the crucified and risen Christ. They need a community that will help them cultivate the courage to embrace their finite, vulnerable humanity. They need a community that will model for them what it means to embrace this temporal existence: to love, to play, to suffer, and to experience profound times of happiness and joy.

So what does WALL-E have to do with Žižek's "monstrosity" and Bonhoeffer's "religionless Christianity"? They all signify an awakening. Žižek sees in the crucified Christ the rupture of every form of ideology that abstracts human identity by rendering human agency impotent. Bonhoeffer interprets the death and resurrection of Jesus Christ as the creation of a new humanity, empowered by the revelation of God's love for the world, to live courageously and responsibly in this world. In WALL-E we find the affirmation of earthly life and the power of relationality and love to awaken and renew human identity. Over and against the abstract, ideal world of the Axiom, WALL-E becomes the "foreign contaminant" that leads to the affirmation of people's finite existence as human creatures.

Reading Bonhoeffer, and reading about Bonhoeffer, it's fascinating to see how the evangelical Christian world has made him into a caricature. He is overwhelmingly known and revered for writing *Discipleship*, the book that he seemed to regret, referring to it as "dangerous." By the end of his short life Bonhoeffer had grown weary of the high-minded principles, morals, and doctrines that Christians used to excuse inaction; he held in disdain the religious principles that rendered the gospel "safe" and "inert." Bonhoeffer appreciated Nietzsche's declaration of the "death of god," not as some atheistic disbelief or nihilism, but the declaration of the end of metaphysics and all reified forms of the "good" or "transcendence" as an affirmation of human life. Bonhoeffer emphatically calls for responsibility, for decision, for action, not based upon some eternal hope, some eternal world beyond, but in the name of a love and way of being revealed in Jesus Christ that is for the world right here and now. For Bonhoeffer this way of life represents the power and courage to stand in the face of death and anxiety, to stare into the darkness of chaos and meaninglessness, and act—to live responsible lives of love and hope. This, I believe, is what youth ministry must become.

Courage and Responsibility: An Example of Religionless Faith

Ben was not a very good high school student. By that I mean he didn't always cooperate with the rules governing the Christian day school he attended. He never did his homework, although he was a very bright and creative young man. He was involved in activities that were forbidden by school policy and by what the community had decided were good Christian morals. He drank alcohol, smoked cigarettes, and skipped class often. He didn't make going to church a habit. It was music that brought Ben and I together; he was in a metal band, and since I played the guitar, he often asked me if I would listen to the new music he had written. During Ben's senior year we played together in a makeshift band for the homecoming pep rally. That spring semester he took a modern US history course I taught, in which we explored the history of rock and roll and critiqued the significant films of the 1950s and '60s. Whereas many students anxiously fretted over issues of doctrine or morality, desperately trying to nail down what it meant to be a Christian, Ben showed no such anxiety. While other students tried to make sure they covered their moral and doctrinal bases while they also participated in the various exploits of youth, Ben had no such concerns: Ben just lived.

A month before graduation we received the horrific news that Ben had died. The rumors swirled as to the cause of death: Was it a drug overdose?

Alcohol? Car accident? The reality was much less exciting but no less tragic: Ben had died of complications from asthma. Because of our relationship his parents asked if I would speak at his memorial service. What struck me about that service was that it included both expressions of grief and moments of laughter and joy. Stories were told about Ben that caught many by surprise. He had a large group of friends and admirers from every social group. Young people spoke of his generosity, how he intentionally included people relegated to the margins. The special education teacher talked about how Ben spent his lunch period sitting and talking with students with special needs. One young man with Down syndrome wept as he spoke of how Ben would take time to talk with him. His parents told stories about a free-spirited kid who loved music, who loved to have a good time, and who loved other people.

As Ben's teacher I had insight into how he articulated his own Christian faith. In a response paper assigned for the film *Lost in Translation,* he wrote of his fears and concerns, but he also wrote about faith. Faith was important to Ben; he believed in God, and he loved Jesus Christ, but he was not much for religion. I read a portion of this assignment at his memorial service and at the end I gave it to his parents. As I handed it to them the look on their face told me that I was not telling them anything new, yet they appreciated having their son's faith shared publicly for others to hear.

Ben exemplifies what Bonhoeffer means when he talks about the presence of Christ at the center of human life that fosters the strength and courage to love our neighbor and embrace this temporal life. I also believe that Ben exemplifies what Bonhoeffer means by "faith" and a "religionless" form of Christianity. Ben had faith; he believed in Jesus, and this belief manifested itself in the love he showed for the people he encountered in all their vulnerability and finitude. However, Ben did not fit the moralistic or doctrinal standards that many in youth ministry use to measure what they consider to be faith. Ben was not interested in living by abstract moral and doctrinal principles. In many ways, Ben, like the young woman (Tiffany) whose clothes and makeup became markers of an absent religiosity, would most likely be labeled as someone for whom faith did not "stick." The truth is Ben's faith did not "stick" as if it were a Post-It Note tacked on to his humanity. Ben's faith in Jesus Christ was at the center of his humanity, demonstrated by his love and concern for concrete human beings and by the manner in which he embraced this temporal life.

So how can Bonhoeffer's "religionless Christianity" speak to the issue of young people leaving the church? More importantly, how can Bonhoeffer's theology help the Christian community develop a posture of ministry that is grounded in the love of God for the world revealed in the death and resurrection of Jesus Christ? The following chapter will address these questions and further explore how Bonhoeffer's "religionless Christianity" provides practical theology with a way to address the issue of young people, faith, and the Christian community.

CHAPTER 6

Faith, Youth, and the Task of the Christian Community

AT THE CENTER OF *WALL-E* is the relationship that develops between WALL-E and EVE. WALL-E falls in love with EVE, and in the end, when she recognizes the depth of WALL-E's sacrifice for her, EVE falls in love with WALL-E. While working to secure the boot plant so EVE can complete her mission, WALL-E is stabbed by AUTO and overwhelmed with electrical current, frying his circuit board. He is left for dead, sent down the garbage shoot to be jettisoned with the rest of the ship's trash. When he is rescued he is near death—the only thing that can save him is to return to his home on earth so he can be rebuilt using his stash of spare parts. As EVE takes action to complete her mission, now driven in part by a desire to save WALL-E, WALL-E helps her complete the mission, but he is crushed in the process.

WALL-E contains obvious echoes of the gospel story. The incarnation, or humanization, of WALL-E reaches its climax in his sacrificial love for EVE and the mission to return the Axiom to earth. WALL-E dies, and in the end he is resurrected—brought back to life by EVE's fast work to reconstruct his circuit board. The story also resonates deeply with Bonhoeffer's theology. For Bonhoeffer, it is the revelation of God's love for the world that is revealed in the death and resurrection of Jesus Christ. It is this revelation of love that opens humanity to love our neighbor and embrace this finite, creaturely life. In other words, it is God's love revealed in Jesus Christ that makes human life possible. All of these movements are reflected in *WALL-E* as WALL-E's sacrifice reveals his love for EVE and his love for the earth.

89

It is this revelation of love that brings restoration and renewal as the love between WALL-E and EVE short-circuits the abstract world of the Axiom and restores humanity to an earthly life.

This story also provides a narrative representation of how the Christian community can respond to the problem of young people leaving the church, by cultivating an expression of love and grace that allows young people to claim their human identity in the context of this earthly life. Rather than respond to this issue out of fear and anxiety by establishing new ways to control or manage the lives of young people, *WALL-E* points to a way of love that helps them claim their finite humanity and embrace an earthly life. Here the gospel proclamation of the death and resurrection of Jesus Christ does not take young people out of the world; instead, it is a response of love and grace that calls young people to embrace life in this world.

An important characteristic of this expression of love is that it is not dependent upon whether young people meet the expectations of the adult world; the love of God revealed in Jesus Christ is without conditions. In other words, young people don't exist for the Christian community—it's not about keeping young people in the church. The Christian community exists to help young people embrace their humanity in the new humanity of Jesus Christ as they live in and for this world. To make this case this chapter will once again turn to the theology of Dietrich Bonhoeffer.

The primary argument of this book is that young people who leave the church are not abandoning faith; they are exchanging one form of faith (orthodox Christianity) for another (Moralistic Therapeutic Deism). Christian Smith's research demonstrates that young people increasingly experience religious belief in the terms of Moral Therapeutic Deism that flows out of the pervasive influence of the consumer society and its powerful hold on the imaginations of young people.

The problem with many of the current attempts to address the issue of young people leaving the church is that they tend to focus on the development of new religious processes without providing a thick description of Christian faith. As the social imaginary of global technocapitalism increasingly becomes the objective reality through which the Christian tradition is mediated, many of these attempts to formulate new processes of faith formation and discipleship are co-opted by the status quo, leaving the fundamental belief structures of the consumer society unnamed and unchallenged. As a result, well-intended attempts to address issues of faith and discipleship end up contributing to the anxious cycle of commodification and abstraction that takes place in Moral Therapeutic Deism.

The last chapter introduced the work of Dietrich Bonhoeffer as the source for an important theological critique of the global technocapitalist ideology and the consumer society. His emphasis upon the crucified and risen Christ as the revelation of God's love for the real world provides an important challenge to the religious function of Moral Therapeutic Deism and the broader consumer society. Bonhoeffer insists that the crucified and resurrected Christ inhabits the center of human life on earth, not some eternal otherworldly heaven, rupturing the reified views of God and humanity by pointing to the revelation of God's love for this finite world. It is this love that establishes the foundation for the Christian community, and it is this love that provides practical theology with the ability to speak to the concrete experience of young people in the West under the pervasive influence of consumer society.

These final two chapters will engage Bonhoeffer's theology as a way to frame the relationship between young people, faith, and the Christian community by providing a thick description of Christian faith as well as the nature and purpose of the Christian community (the church). These definitions will help the community as it engages the lived experience of young people as they are shaped by the social imaginary of global technocapitalism and consumer society. Finally, I will argue that Bonhoeffer's theology makes possible a poetic form of youth ministry that hermeneutically "remythologizes" the world through the gospel proclamation of the death and resurrection of Jesus Christ. It is in the context of the two poles of "religionlessness" and "remythologization" that the Christian community can begin to formulate a response to the issue of young people and faith grounded in the proclamation of the gospel.

The Conformation of Faith

A crucial part of the response to the issue of young people leaving the church is a thick description of what we mean by "faith." Often, this issue is referred to as a crisis of faith, or even a loss of faith; yet, little attention is given to defining what we mean. This lack of definition leads to uncertainty about the source and content of faith. Is faith something that humans produce through processes and techniques? Or is faith a gift given by God through the Holy Spirit? What difference does it make?

As described above, Bonhoeffer sees faith as a way of knowing that opens individuals to receive the revelation of God in the person of Jesus Christ. The Holy Spirit is the one who establishes the conditions for faith, preparing the space for an encounter with the divine "other" in Jesus Christ that opens humanity to be able to love God and neighbor. This revelatory encounter liberates humanity from the closed cycle of violence and control caused by sin and makes possible a way of life grounded in the new humanity of Jesus Christ. Faith, for Bonhoeffer, is what makes the relationship between God and humanity possible, creating the conditions for a new way of being in the world.

At the center of faith—what some might call the "object" of faith—is the crucified and risen Christ in whom the identity of God and what it means to be human are revealed. For Bonhoeffer, it is to this revealed reality that humanity and the world must conform. As discussed above, Bonhoeffer maintains that humanity exists either in the being of Adam (fallen humanity) or in the being of Jesus Christ (new humanity). The being of Adam is characterized by the knowledge of good and evil, which Bonhoeffer describes as the human tendency to bring all things, including God, under the control of human rationality and consciousness.[1] After the fall all of humanity shares in the being of Adam, characterized by the sinful curvature of the self (Augustine and Luther).[2] Only through the revelation of Jesus Christ do we become aware of our sinful condition, and it is only by faith that we are transformed into a new form of humanity that is grounded in Jesus Christ.[3] For Bonhoeffer, faith is not a process of becoming like Christ through methods or programs; faith is an objective reality that is revealed in Jesus Christ. This means that being in Christ is not a possibility,

---

1. Bonhoeffer, *Creation and Fall*, 116. Bonhoeffer writes, "Thus for their knowledge of God human beings renounce the life that comes from this word and grab it for themselves. They themselves stand in the center. This is disobedience in the semblance of obedience, the desire to rule in the semblance of service, the will to be creator in the semblance of being a creature, being dead in the semblance of life." Ibid. Subsequently referred to as *DBWE* 3.

2. Bonhoeffer, *Act and Being*, 137 (subsequently referred to as *DBWE* 2). Bonhoeffer writes, "For 'in Adam' means to be in untruth, in culpable perversion of the will, that is, of human essence. It means to be turned inward into one's self, *cor curvum in se*." Ibid.

3. Ibid., 136. Bonhoeffer writes, "Were it really a human possibility for persons themselves to know that they are sinners apart from revelation, neither 'being in Adam' nor 'being in Christ would be existential designations of their being. For it would mean that human beings could place themselves into the truth, that they could somehow withdraw to a deeper being of their own . . ." Ibid.

nor is it something that humans produce; being in Christ is an objective reality accomplished only by the work of Jesus Christ. There is no process of becoming like Christ; there is only the actualization of the reality of the new humanity in a community characterized by love. Either we are, or are not, "in Christ"—there's no in-between.

This distinction is important because it establishes that faith is not something that is created or grown by human methods. Bonhoeffer is adamant that the purpose of the Christian life is not to become "like Jesus" through formulaic methods or religious processes. God is the one who creates faith through the Holy Spirit, which leads to the reality of Christ's new humanity becoming actualized in history through a community of love. Bonhoeffer writes:

> This does not happen as we strive "to become like Jesus," as we customarily say, but as the form of Jesus Christ himself so works on us that it molds us, conforming our form to Christ's own . . . Christ remains the only one who forms. Christian people do not form the world with their ideas. Rather, Christ forms human beings to a form the same as Christ's own. However, just as the form of Christ is misperceived where he is understood essentially as the teacher of a pious and good life, so formation of human beings is also wrongly understood where one sees it only as guidance for a pious and good life.[4]

Bonhoeffer is suspicious of what he refers to as "so-called practical Christianity" and he is adamant that the focus of Scripture is not the "formation of the world by planning and programs." He writes, "This does not mean that the teachings of Christ or so-called Christian principles should be applied directly to the world in order to form the world according to them. Formation occurs only by being drawn into the form of Jesus Christ, by being conformed to the unique form of the one who became human, was crucified and is risen."[5]

Bonhoeffer insists that pious practices do not build or grow faith; these methods do not make faith "stick." Using this language brings God under the control and management of human rationality and consciousness. Bonhoeffer argues that it is through faith that we are conformed to the new humanity revealed in Jesus Christ, and this is solely the work of Christ alone.

4. *DBWE* 6:91–92.
5. Ibid., 92.

This understanding of faith as conformation challenges every attempt to make faith into an objective form of revelation or spiritual method, whether it is doctrine, the institutional church, spiritual practices, or even the Bible. It opposes every attempt to conflate God's action with human methods, which Bonhoeffer expresses this way:

> [T]he view that interprets revelation as something that exists implies that human beings can freely and at all times have recourse to this existing something, which one comes across.... It is at their disposal, whether in terms of religious experience, the verbally inspired Bible, or the Catholic church. They know themselves held secure, borne by this something that exists (even though such securing can consist only in that human beings remain by themselves, precisely because the existing something as such is given over into their power).[6]

This view of faith is grounded in the Protestant understanding of justification that emphasizes the vicarious work of Christ's death and resurrection that restores and actualizes the relationship between God and humanity in the creation of a community of love—the church. Christian faith establishes the conditions for the revelation of the crucified and risen Christ and the new humanity—the Christian community—that functions as a sign of God's love for the world. It is this community that proclaims the love of God for the world and testifies to the formation of the world to the image of Jesus Christ.

Bonhoeffer and the Church

Bonhoeffer is careful to differentiate the church and faith from religion. In *Sanctorum Communio* Bonhoeffer writes, "God established the reality of the church, of humanity pardoned in Jesus Christ—not religion, but revelation, not religious community, but church. This is what the reality of Jesus Christ means."[7] He makes this distinction because it is essential to recognize that the inner logic of the church is based upon revelation (faith) not religion (reified principles of human reason and consciousness). Because the revelation of God in Jesus Christ is fundamentally social, the content of this revelation leads to the formation of a community in the world that is the presence of God's love in the world. Bonhoeffer summarizes it this

6. *DBWE* 2:108.
7. *DBWE* 1:153.

—Faith, Youth, and the Task of the Christian Community—

way: "In Christ God loves human beings and opens the divine heart; and in giving God's own self to sinful human beings God renews them at the same time and thus makes the new community possible and real; but this means that God's love wills community."[8]

The church, for Bonhoeffer, is the concrete community in which the new humanity of Jesus Christ is made present in the world. The essence of this community, according to Bonhoeffer, is demonstrated in the act of being with and for the "other" in three primary ways: "self-renouncing, active work for their neighbor; intercessory prayer; and, finally, the mutual forgiveness of sins in God's name."[9] The fundamental task of the church, which flows from the social nature of the community, is to intercede for our neighbor, which means that the Christian community exists not for its own sake, but for the sake of the world. Bonhoeffer writes, "In intercession the nature of Christian love again proves to be to work 'with,' 'for,' and ultimately 'in place of' our neighbor, thereby drawing the neighbor deeper and deeper into the church-community."[10]

This interpretation of the church as the concrete community of love in and for the world is the context for Bonhoeffer's vision of "religionless Christianity." "Religionless" does not mean the absence or abandonment of beliefs or practice; rather, it is a call for the community to take seriously its ethical responsibility for the neighbor and for the world. Bonhoeffer realized that the West was increasingly shaped not by religion, but by secularity. His primary concern in calling for a "religionless" form of Christianity was to pose the question "Who is Jesus Christ?" for those who no longer think in the categories of religion. Bonhoeffer understood that the pressing issues facing the West were no longer described in religious language, but in the languages of science and secularity. Yet, even as the religious forms and questions dissipated, Bonhoeffer insisted that the Christian community remain within the world, not on the edges, but at the center, called into responsibility with and for the world. Bonhoeffer writes, "What matters is not the beyond but this world, how it is created and preserved, is given laws, reconciled, and renewed. What is beyond this world is meant, in the gospel, to be there for this world—not in the anthropocentric sense of liberal,

---

8. Ibid., 173.
9. Ibid., 184.
10. Ibid., 189.

mystical, pietistic, ethical theology, but in the biblical sense of the creation and the incarnation, crucifixion, and resurrection of Jesus Christ."[11]

Bonhoeffer's ultimate concern is the meaning of the revelation of God in Jesus Christ for this life in this world. He does not reject belief in bodily resurrection or a future life, but he does oppose every form of religion that denigrates and cheapens this finite created existence by appealing to abstract forms of "eternity." With the decline of religion, and the rise of secularity, Bonhoeffer does not question the existence of the church, he does not even call into question the practices of the church, but he asks what form it will take within the world "come of age."

The Christian community must ask this same question as it addresses the lived experience of young people living in the West. Many young people are leaving the church in response to the shift in social imaginary and the disintegration of the world view that used to sustain traditional forms of Christian belief. Increasingly, the social imaginaries of young people are being shaped by the new economic and political patterns of global techno-capitalism that have developed because of the shift from a producer society to a consumer society. This new cultural experience represents a shift in how sovereign power is understood and applied, moving from the radical transcendence of a supernatural world view to the immanent expressions of power in the economic and political spheres. This transformation gives rise to the consumer society and the religious function of Moral Therapeutic Deism, complete with its own narratives of sin and redemption, and its own articulation of transcendence. Given this religious function of the consumer society, with its emphasis upon abstraction and reification, Bonhoeffer's critique of religion applies just as much today as it did in the mid-twentieth century. His question concerning the nature and form of the church in the "world come of age" is the fundamental question for the church today as it addresses the crisis of young people leaving the church. More specifically, the question for those who work with young people is this: What does youth ministry look like in a "world come of age"?

The Reality of the Church

For Bonhoeffer, the church is the concrete, historical community that makes the love of God for the world revealed in Jesus Christ a present reality. The church is grounded in sociality, which means that the church is a historical

11. *DBWE* 8:373.

sign of the new humanity of Jesus Christ in which we are able to love God and our neighbor. As discussed above, it is important to recognize that, for Bonhoeffer, that the church is not a possibility; the church is an objective reality in Jesus Christ.[12] Recognizing this prevents the Christian community from becoming obsessed with its own preservation. The church is created by the revelation of God's love for the world in Jesus Christ, which means the existence of the church is grounded in God's action, not human action. The church, as it exists at different times and within different cultures, is a historical sign of God's love for the world. This means that the community must be careful it does not becomes so anxious that it overemphasizes the imperfections and problems that develop within the community. Yes—the church should take steps to address problems and issues that arise within the community; at the same time, Bonhoeffer insists that the historical reality of the church has taken, and will continue to take, many different forms as it is constantly renewed.[13] The primary concern of the Christian community must not be about ensuring its preservation; the church must be focused upon its proper task. Bonhoeffer writes, "In sticking to its calling—that is, preaching the risen Jesus Christ—the church deals a deadly blow to the spirit of annihilation. . . .The church makes clear with its message of the living Lord Jesus Christ, however, that it is not simply concerned with preserving what has been handed down from the past. It forces the custodians of power in particular to listen and change their ways."[14]

The primary task of the church is to communicate the revelation of God in Jesus Christ to and for the world. This is a hermeneutical task by which the church performs and lives into its identity as the new humanity of Jesus Christ in the world in every historical and cultural moment. For Bonhoeffer, this happens as we love our neighbor, because in loving our neighbor the love of God in Jesus Christ becomes a historical reality, opening the world to encounter transcendence. The goal of loving our neighbor

---

12. *DBWE* 1:153. Bonhoeffer writes, "The relationship of Jesus Christ to the Christian church is thus to be understood in a dual sense. (1) *The church is already completed in Christ, time suspended.* (2) *The church is to be built within time upon Christ as the firm foundation. Christ is the historical principle of the church.*" Ibid.

13. Ibid., 231. Bonhoeffer discusses the importance of the institutional church and what he calls "house churches" for the life of the church. He writes, "The growth of both forms ought to go hand in hand. Attempts at church renewal, such as the Pietist community movement, ought to increase rather than sap the lifeblood from the institutional church." Ibid.

14. *DBWE* 6:132.

is not to preserve the community—it's not to make sure young people come to church; for Bonhoeffer, the "purpose of love is exclusively determined by God's will for the other person, namely, to subject the other to God's rule."[15]

The focus of Christian love is not to coerce the neighbor into becoming part of the community, nor is it to make sure that particular historical or cultural versions of the community exist for all eternity. To focus on these things is to fall into the trap of reifying a particular version of the church, whether it is the institution, specific doctrines, or certain practices and belief systems. Instead, the love practiced by the Christian community is directed outward, for the sake of the world, so that the world might encounter the love of God revealed in the person of Jesus Christ.

For Bonhoeffer, the love that is grounded in Christian faith is a love for the "real" neighbor. It is not conditioned by principles or ideals; it is a love that "knows no limits," seeking God's rule in "each and every place."[16] Bonhoeffer writes, "Love for our neighbor is our will to embrace God's will for the other person; God's will for the other person is defined for us in the unrestricted command to surrender our self centered will to our neighbor, which neither means to love the other instead of God, nor to love God in the other, but to put the other in our own place and to love the neighbor instead of ourselves."[17]

The Christian community becomes a historical reality by loving the neighbor as a sign of the reality and presence of the new humanity revealed in Jesus Christ—a sign that reveals the truth about what it means to be a human being. Bonhoeffer writes:

> Jesus was not the individual who sought to achieve some personal perfection, but only lived as the one who in himself has taken on and bears the selves of all human beings. His entire living, acting, and suffering was vicarious representative action [*Stellvertretung*]. All that human beings were supposed to live, do, and suffer was fulfilled in him. In this real vicarious representative action, in which his human existence consists, he is the responsible human being par excellence. . . . As vicariously representative life and action, responsibility is essentially a relation from one human being to another. Christ became human, and thus bore vicarious representative responsibility for all human beings.[18]

15. *DBWE* 1:168.
16. Ibid., 170.
17. Ibid., 172.
18. *DBWE* 6:258–59.

In Jesus Christ the true nature of humanity is shown to be not an abstract, ideal form of humanity, but a concrete ethical responsibility that responds to the claim our neighbor makes on us. In this way, the neighbor functions as a limit, a presence that demands a response. The question is, what type of response will we give? One that seeks to violate the limit by violently controlling or naming my neighbor, or one that is open to the neighbor as other in grace and love? The historical presence of the Christian community is a sign of a new way of being human that is grounded in the love of God for the world, which makes possible a love of neighbor that is grounded in the call to ethical responsibility in Jesus Christ.

For Bonhoeffer, the humanity that is revealed in Jesus Christ is a humanity that is set free to be the "creature of the Creator." He writes, "Pretension, hypocrisy, compulsion, forcing oneself to be something different, better, more ideal than one is—all are abolished. God loves the real human being. God became a real human being."[19] This, for Bonhoeffer, is the humanizing task of the church. The church is "nothing but that piece of humanity where Christ has taken form. . . . The Church is the human being who has become human, has been judged, and has been awakened to new life."[20] The task of the Christian community is to proclaim the restoration of the relationship between God and humanity that sets the world free from all dehumanizing and objectifying abstractions, principles, and ideals. For Bonhoeffer, this includes being set free from the religious processes used to control and domesticate humanity, which means that the task of the community is not to call the world back into moral, ethical, or religious abstraction or burden the world with doctrines or principles. Instead, the task of the church is to testify to the true, concrete humanity revealed in Jesus Christ. This is the function and task of the church in *Sanctorum Communio*, and this remains the purpose and task of the church in Bonhoeffer's *Letters and Papers*. What changes for Bonhoeffer are the historical conditions in which the community lives and proclaims the gospel.

What This Means for Young People

Bonhoeffer's definitions of faith and the task of the church provide an important starting point from which to address the issues of young people, faith, and the church. Bonhoeffer's theology insists that the church must

19. Ibid., 94.
20. Ibid., 97.

not approach this issue from a posture of fear that tries to protect and preserve current historical versions of the church. These attempts inevitably become a form of idealist reification in which we make the church in our image through a strong theological emphasis upon doctrinal and institutional principles. This usually results in an overemphasis on doctrinal "orthodoxy" and purity that cuts the church off from the world. It often includes the reification of the Bible, doctrine, and the institutional church as objective propositions of absolute truth. This perspective also has the tendency to disconnect matters of Christian faith from the issues of cultural life, as eternity, spirituality, and the holy become principles that relegate temporal, created life as something less real. Consequently, the joys and suffering of this life are not taken seriously as ethical responsibility gives way to maintaining truth and adhering to higher spiritual and theological principles. The church in this context becomes inwardly and upwardly focused and is no longer able to speak to the historical and cultural experiences of young people. At the same time, the inability to recognize the culturally conditional, historical nature of the church means that a specific cultural paradigm is reified and held up to be the holy, absolute truth for all times and places.

The consequence of this type of sectarian approach for young people is that they become cut off from the experience of temporal, finite, human existence as they come under the influence of static institutional and doctrinal systems that present God and human nature as an unattainable ideal. The inability to attain these ideals leads to a variety of reactions. Young people either choose to disassociate from the world and the imperfect experiences of temporal finitude, or they choose a bifurcated approach to religion in which the temporal, lived experience of the world is disconnected from religious belief. Another possibility, which is in line with the research discussed above, is becoming more of an option: young people reject Christianity in favor of the lived experience of the secular life.

The flip side of this defensive posture is the attempt of the church to accommodate the Christian tradition to the changing cultural paradigms. Here, the cultural paradigms of modernity and postmodernity are taken to be the objective truth about the world. Kinnaman's *You Lost Me*, for example, argues that the church must update its beliefs and practices in order to bring them in line with the experiences of young people. In the introduction he emphasizes the need to "reimagine faith and practice" for the purpose of discipling the next generation for Jesus.[21] While Kinnaman would not self-identify with "liberal theology," this is ultimately where his position leads. Kinnaman's project reifies the cultural paradigms young people inhabit, taking them for granted as the truth about the world by calling the church to bring its theology and practice in line with cultural principles. Faith is "reimagined" in a way that brings revelation under the control of abstract, rational principles accessible to human consciousness. Even if it is unintentional, Kinnaman falls into this trap, in part, because he does not define what he means by faith, the church, and discipleship.

Here, again, Bonhoeffer's definition of faith, and his articulation of the nature and task of the church, provide an important critique of this approach. As previously discussed, Bonhoeffer rejects any type of accommodation of faith, and the Christian community, to cultural paradigms because this places revelation under the power of human action and consciousness. This approach does not lead to a true experience of God or transcendence; it leads instead to the reification of cultural ideals and principles that leaves humanity trapped within a closed system of thought.

Bonhoeffer believes the church must stay focused on its primary task: to live as the sign of God's love for the world revealed in Jesus Christ by loving our neighbor. This understanding of the church's mission and task recognizes the hermeneutical function of the community to communicate the reality of God's love for the world, revealed in the death and resurrection of Jesus Christ, within each historical and cultural moment. This means that the focus of the Christian community should not be how to keep young people in the church, nor is it creating or adapting processes and techniques to grow or reimagine faith. The task of the church is to be the sign and presence of God's love for young people within their historical and cultural experience.

This is not to say that the practice of the community is unimportant. The church will always be a place in which liturgical practice (namely the preaching of the word, the sacraments, and forgiveness of sin), various modes of pastoral care, and creative methods of passing on the tradition through catechesis and education occur. An important part of the church's task is to be a gathering where the community confesses a common faith in

---

21. Kinnaman and Hawkins, *You Lost Me*, 12. Kinnaman writes, "From this generation, so intent on reimagining faith and practice, I believe the established church can learn new patterns of faithfulness. *You Lost Me* seeks to explain the next generation's cultural context and examine the question *How can we follow Jesus—and help young people faithfully follow Jesus—in a dramatically changing culture?*" Ibid.

Jesus Christ. However, this confession of faith, for Bonhoeffer, must never be confused with religious processes. He writes, "Confession of faith is not to be confused with professing a religion. Such profession uses the confession as propaganda and ammunition against the Godless. The confession of faith belongs rather to the 'Discipline of the Secret' (Arkanum) in the Christian gathering of those who believe. . . . The primary confession of the Christian before the world is the deed which interprets itself. If the deed is to have become a force, then the world itself will long to confess the Word."[22]

The primary task and responsibility of the Christian community for young people is not to burden them with new forms of orthodoxy or positivistic views of the Bible, doctrine, or the institutional church, nor is it to accommodate the Christian belief to the discourses of contemporary culture. The primary task of the community is to be the sign and presence of God's love for the world revealed in Jesus Christ within the contemporary lived experience of young people.

For Bonhoeffer, this means that the Christian community must become responsible for young people as they live within the oppressive and dehumanizing consumer society under the influence of the global technocapitalist ideology. It means entering into their guilt, their suffering, and their objectified commodification in the name of the crucified Christ, while testifying to and performing the new humanity that has come into the world in Christ's resurrection. It is through this double movement of presence and performance that the love of God in Jesus Christ is made known to young people, opening them to the possibility of a new way of being in the world. All this leads to the question: What does this look like?

Youth Ministry as Responsible Ethical Action: An Example

Recently, I heard the story of a young man who experienced a mental breakdown. He was academically gifted, an excellent athlete, and he came from a prominent wealthy family. In every part of life he had the necessary tools and connections to be successful within consumer society. A mental breakdown brought all of this crashing down. He was hospitalized for a short time and diagnosed with bipolar disorder. His new lived reality

---

22. Bonhoeffer, Kelly, and Nelson, *Testament to Freedom*, 86. See also *DBWE* 8:373, where Bonhoeffer writes, "That means an 'arcane discipline' must be reestablished, though which the mysteries of the Christian faith are sheltered against profanation."

brought manic episodes, dark depression, and crippling social anxiety. His medication left him drowsy and unmotivated, and he had a difficult time making ordinary, everyday decisions he used to take for granted.

As he experienced his first episode of crisis he reached out to a youth pastor with whom he had a prior relationship. The nature of their relationship was pastoral, but it did not involve prayer, Scripture reading, or formal pastoral counseling. The focus of their relationship was helping this young man acclimate to his new reality. The youth pastor went with him to therapy sessions and helped him begin to work through his social anxiety by going with him into grocery stores and public places. This youth pastor used his connections in the Christian community to help the young man find employment; he helped him find an affordable car to drive, and an apartment to rent. He listened as this young man lamented his feelings of loneliness and embarrassment; he listened as this young man talked about the pain he caused his family and how he felt despair about his future. Much of their time was spent engaged in small talk about sports teams over burgers and cheap cigars. Nothing was said about going to church or pious spiritual practices, and nothing was said about reading the Bible or praying. Everything was focused upon helping this young man begin to renarrate his life.

To the broader culture this young man was a failed commodity—ejected from the networks that promised him a successful life. This youth pastor dared to love him by entering into his experience of mental illness. He took responsibility for this young man by entering into his darkness and despair, not for the purpose of trying to convert him, but for the purpose of speaking into his life the new humanity of the crucified and resurrected Christ. This, I believe, is an example of what it means for the Christian community to take responsibility for young people within the social and cultural world of global technocapitalism.

The Earth Remains Our Mother

Bonhoeffer's work provides a powerful theological perspective to help equip the Christian community to take responsibility for young people caught within the objectifying abstraction of global technocapitalism and the consumer society. As technocapitalism becomes further entrenched, the endless cycle of making and remaking oneself into a commodity will become more pervasive. The ever-fluctuating networks mean that the line separating insiders from those who are ejected as "failed commodities" will continue to change—excluding an increasing number of young people from the "system." It is into this social and cultural reality that Bonhoeffer's theology speaks a prophetic word concerning God's love for real humanity in the person of Jesus Christ, revealing a new way of being in the world that cannot be reduced to techniques and processes.

Bonhoeffer testifies to the presence of God in the crucified Christ, a revelation that subverts every form of idealized humanity and every attempt to transcend the human condition through processes of perfection and improvement. He proclaims the hope of Christ's resurrection as the revelation of God's love and embrace of real humanity that is meant to live in this world. Bonhoeffer provides a theological language that challenges the "religious" tendencies within the church as it unmasks the influence of the global technocapitalist social imaginary on the lives of young people in the West.

These religious tendencies can be seen in the way churches and youth programs anxiously fill the space by trying to manage the spiritual lives of young people with programs and service projects. The focus of this filling is production, growth, and improvement under the labels of piety, discipleship, and faith formation. Every experience, every lesson, every small group is supposed to lead to an encounter with transcendence in which young people strengthen their faith. The problem with this approach is that the objective reality inscribed within the identity of young people is increasingly shaped by the pragmatic, process-driven perspective of technocapitalism. Thus, to possess true Christian faith is equated with a spiritual desire for piety, Scripture reading, and prayer that leads to recognizable (measurable) growth.

One afternoon I had a student stop by my office to talk about something with which he was struggling. He proceeded to beat himself up because he wasn't praying enough, he wasn't reading Scripture enough, and he had fallen away from what he referred to as "practices of discipleship." After listening to him for awhile, I opened up about my own devotional life. "I don't have one," I told him. "I hate devotional reading, I stink at prayer, and I really don't feel like reading my Bible." The student stared back at me, stunned. "When I do pray," I continued, "I usually use liturgical prayers because otherwise I'm not going to pray. I go to church on Sunday, listen to the sermon, and say the creed, not because I want to, or because I feel like it. I do these things not because I have it all figured out, I do them because I have doubts. I pray, read the Bible, and go to church because I want to believe. Maybe you should cut yourself some slack; you are only human after all." His response indicated a sense of relief, not because he fully agreed with me (he didn't), but because he appreciated hearing someone give him permission to let go of the anxious desire to constantly live up to the religious expectations of the community.

The significance of Bonhoeffer's theology for the church is that it calls us out from anxiety and religious processes so that we might claim a life of faith grounded in our concrete human condition in Jesus Christ. Of course, for Bonhoeffer, the Christian life is a call to a form of discipleship that is not weak or "cheap," but is demanding and costly precisely because it is a call to embrace our human condition.[23] Thus, for Bonhoeffer, true faith is not about processes or principles, and it is not the absence of doubt. True faith means confessing the creed in the midst of our own unbelief, as we embrace the concrete complexities of temporal life. So how does the church confront the religious tendencies of the technocapitalist paradigm? We do this by giving young people the space to doubt, to ask questions, and to confess what they believe in the midst of their unbelief.

Bonhoeffer also provides the Christian community with the language needed to help young people take responsibility for this life. Faith, for Bonhoeffer, does not take us out of this world and into a world of eternal principles; faith it is a call to live as the new humanity within the concrete situations of this earthly existence. In his lecture "What Is a Christian Ethic?," Bonhoeffer challenges the Christian community to live into the complexities of this world.[24] He writes:

> The profound old saga tells of the giant Antaeus, who was stronger than any man on earth; no one could overcome him until once in a fight someone lifted him from the ground; then the giant lost all the strength which had flowed into him through his contact to with the earth. We who would leave the earth, who would depart form the present distress, lose the power which still holds us by eternal, mysterious forces. The earth remains our mother, just as God remains our Father, and our mother will only lay in the Father's arms those who remain true to her. That is the Christian's song of earth and her distress.[25]

---

23. Bonhoeffer, *Discipleship*, 4.
24. Bonhoeffer, Kelly, and Nelson, *Testament to Freedom*, 351.
25. Ibid.

Faith in Jesus Christ, in this context, is about having the strength and courage to live into this embodied, temporal life. It means to take seriously the joy and sorrow of this life, to own it, and to experience it fully. Faith, for Bonhoeffer, represents the courage to live an earthly life without having to resort to eternal principles for meaning and purpose. Bonhoeffer poses the question "Who stands fast?" He responds by emphasizing that it is not those who adhere to "conscience" or "higher virtue"—those who appeal to some reified abstraction as the source of their identity and action. It is "only the one who is prepared to sacrifice all of these when, in faith and in relationships to God alone, he is called to obedient and responsible action."[26] For Bonhoeffer, it is in the ability to love and embrace this earthly life and creaturely existence that a person begins to "believe in the resurrection of the dead and a new world."[27]

Once, I was asked to speak to a group of sixth and seventh graders on the issue of human identity and Christian faith, so I used the film *WALL-E* get the conversation started. When I asked for their initial thoughts they began to use biblical and spiritual language like "made in God's image," "moral," "sinful," and "soul" or "spirit." Finally, I stopped and said, "Really? These are the first things you think about?" So I asked about our bodily functions, opposable thumbs, our ability to create culture, or the fact that we are relational and wired for friendship. This led to a hilarious discussion about the distinction between "imperfection" and "sin."

When I asked them why we do things like work, play, or even establish friendships and families, the answers they gave once again focused upon religious principles they had learned, like "the glory of God" or "God's will." I responded by suggesting that maybe we do these things because we enjoy doing them, and maybe God loves that we enjoy doing them. I suggested we do these things because that is what humans do, and that is what we are meant to do. I then suggested that maybe the purpose of life is not to die and go to heaven, but that the purpose of life is to live and embrace this temporal, embodied existence. The place erupted. Not because they were angry, although a few of them were, but because they had so many questions. Many of them had never entertained the idea that this embodied life might have its own value apart from the life to come. One reason for this is that young people are so engrained to think in the terms of surplus value, that activities are only meaningful if we meet a goal or receive some

26. *DBWE* 8:40.
27. Ibid., 213.

reward. Many of them couldn't wrap their minds around the possibility that temporal, ordinary life might be good and meaningful. I did clarify that my point was not to deny the life to come, but that the life to come might look and feel a lot like this life, which is a good thing. Needless to say, not everyone was convinced as they left.

If I had more time I would have brought up Bonhoeffer's argument that grounding the meaning of life in abstract religious principles causes us to take God and the world "less" seriously. The majority of young people at this event would have disagreed because for them nothing is more seriously than acknowledging "God's will" or "eternal life." What they fail to recognize, however, is that this religious or principled approach ends up pushing God to the edges of life. God, for Bonhoeffer, becomes the deus ex machina who breaks in when things go wrong, or, as with the young people engaged in this discussion, God provides the basis for meaning when our human attempts fail.[28] This is why Bonhoeffer calls for an end to religion, because it is grounded in anxiety and fear; whereas faith in Jesus Christ flows from the center of human life that is grounded in courage and strength.[29]

The current crisis of young people, faith, and their relationship to the Christian community is closely related to the anxiety that Bonhoeffer describes. Not only are the lives of young people constantly under the threat of being objectified and commodified within the global technocapitalist system, but they also face the anxiety of the Christian community that desperately tries to keep young people in the church through an onslaught of religious processes and principles. As the work of Charles Taylor and Philip Goodchild demonstrate, this struggle for the hearts and minds of young people is fundamentally religious in nature. The new economic and political processes that make up global technocapitalism represent new forms of sovereign power and transcendence that developed with the secularization of Western culture. The response of the Christian community to this new religious and cultural situation has been to develop new forms of religious processes and techniques. In the end, however, these practices are co-opted by the consumer society as Christian belief is accommodated to the ideology of the broader social and cultural paradigm.

Bonhoeffer's religionless Christianity provides the Christian community with an approach to this issue. It is a theological response, grounded in the crucified and resurrected Christ, that is less concerned with the

---

28. Ibid., 281.
29. Ibid., 282.

preservation of the church and more focused on expressing God's love for young people in concrete ways. It is a response that seeks to humanize young people in the context of the new humanity made present in the world through love. It is a response that declares God's love for the world by helping young people cultivate the strength and courage to embrace this finite, temporal human life. It is a response that does not rely on principles, processes, or programs; it is a poetic response that redescribes the world young people inhabit in the context of the death and resurrection of Jesus Christ.

Poetically Re-Describing the World

A poetic approach to Christian faith is fundamentally a hermeneutical encounter in which meaning and knowledge are conveyed through the act of interpretation. In his book *What Would Jesus Deconstruct?: The Good News of Postmodernism for the Church,* John Caputo refers to the New Testament as an act of "theo-poetics" or the "poetics of the Kingdom of God." He writes, "From a work such as that we cannot simply and straightforwardly 'derive' a course of action. We need instead to 'arrive' at an instantiation, a concretization, a way to translate it into existence, all the while letting it happen (*arriver*) to us, allowing ourselves to come under its spell and be transformed by the event it harbors."[30]

Caputo argues that the Christian community lives in the world haunted by the "dangerous memory" of the death and resurrection of Jesus Christ—a memory that unsettles every attempt to name the truth about the world.[31] At the same time, the Christian community is called to action in the world—what Caputo refers to as a Kierkegaardian leap—recognizing that our action never fully realizes the kingdom of God in the world because the kingdom never fully arrives.[32] Thus, it is both the memory and future hope of the event of the kingdom of God that calls the Christian community to responsible action in and for the world, not by making Christian faith into absolute truth, but by being pried open to the call of the

---

30. Caputo, *What Would Jesus Deconstruct?*

31. Ibid., 61. Caputo writes, "That is a notion that is profoundly rich in its implications for Christianity, which is organized around its own *memoria passionis*: the memory of the passion of Jesus, which Metz calls the 'dangerous memories of the sufferings of Jesus.'" Ibid.

32. Ibid., 68.

— Faith, Youth, and the Task of the Christian Community —

"event"—the call of the crucified and resurrected Christ. Here we find that Caputo's "theo-poetics" provides an important way to frame Bonhoeffer's "religionless Christianity" as the poetic weakening of every human attempt to objectify and reify God and humanity.

As Bonhoeffer makes the case for "religionlessness" Christianity he appeals to the work of Rudolf Bultmann and his project of "demythologization." He writes, "A few more words about 'religionlessness.' You probably remember Bultmann's essay on 'demythologizing' the New Testament. My opinion of it today would be that he went not 'too far,' as most people thought, but rather not far enough. It's not only 'mythological' concepts like miracles, ascension, and so on (which in principle can't be separated from concepts of God, faith, etc.!) that are problematic, but 'religious' concepts as such. You can't separate God from the miracles (as Bultmann thinks); instead, you must be able to interpret and proclaim them both 'nonreligiously.'"[33]

In a prior letter written in 1942, Bonhoeffer affirms Bultmann's project when he writes:

> Now as to Bultmann I belong to those who welcomed his writing—not because I agree with it. I regret the twofold approach it takes.... In this regard perhaps I have remained Harnack's student to this day. To put it bluntly: Bultmann has let the cat out of the bag, not only for himself but for a great many people (the liberal cat out of the confessional bag), and in this I rejoice. He has dared to say what many repress in themselves (here I include myself) without having overcome it. He thereby has rendered a service to intellectual integrity and honesty. Many brothers oppose him with a hypocritical faith and that I find deadly. Now an account must be given. I would like to speak with Bultmann about this and open myself to the fresh air that comes from him. But then the window has to be shut again. Otherwise the susceptible will too easily catch a cold.[34]

If this statement is taken apart from the rest of his work it is easy to understand why Bonhoeffer has at times been accused of advocating for a demythologized Christianity as a way to speak of God and faith in the secularized West. Certainly, Bonhoeffer's "religionless" impulse, and his affinity for Bultmann's project of demythologization, represents an iconoclastic

---

33. *DBWE* 8:372.
34. Bonhoeffer and Brocker, *Conspiracy and Imprisonment*, 347.

impulse directed at the religious and ethical abstractions he strongly opposed. However, in a well-known letter written in June 1944, Bonhoeffer engages the question of the relationship between Christ and the "world come of age" by critiquing Bultmann. He writes:

> As for Bultmann, he seems to have sensed Barth's limitations somehow, but misunderstands it in the sense of liberal theology, and thus falls into typical liberal reductionism (the "mythological" elements in Christianity are taken out, thus reducing Christianity to its "essence"). My view, however, is that the full content, including the "mythological" concepts, must remain—the New Testament is not a mythological dressing up of a universal truth, but this mythology (resurrection and so forth) is the thing itself!—but that these concepts must now be interpreted in a way that does not make religion the condition for faith.[35]

This mythological affirmation suggests a two-part movement within Bonhoeffer's project of "religionless Christianity." The first is the iconoclastic move of the cross in which every form of idealist abstraction and every oppressive form of reification is negated, freeing the world and humanity to become the creation and creature that God intends for it to be. In other words, Bonhoeffer believes the cross of Jesus Christ ruptures or weakens every expression of strong theology that tries to say with absolute certainty the truth about the world. For Bonhoeffer, the project of demythologization not only applies to Scripture or theology, but it also applies to the ideological and religious functions of culture that control and dehumanize.

This "demythologization" of the cross is followed by a second move grounded in resurrection that "remythologizes" the world according to the revelation of God in Jesus Christ and the presence of the new humanity existing in and for the world. This second move establishes a poetic ontology that guards against a continued process of reification and abstraction. Thus, this poetic remythologization of the world in Jesus Christ is not a reenchantment of the world but a redescription of the world that opens it to a new reality and the possibility of a new future in Jesus Christ.

This reading of Bonhoeffer's "religionless Christianity" resonates with the hermeneutical work of Paul Ricoeur regarding truth, metaphor, and the poetic.[36] "Metaphor," according to Ricoeur, disrupts and ruptures the

---

35. *DBWE* 8:430.

36. For a conversation on the hermeneutical nature of Bonhoeffer's work, see Gregor and Zimmerman, *Bonhoeffer and Continental Thought*.

"old order" and brings forth a new one, which results in the creation of new meaning by redescribing reality. Ricoeur argues for the power of the poetic to initiate a process of iconoclasm and new creation. He writes:

> A second line of reflection seems to be suggested by the idea of categorical transgression, understood as deviation in relation to pre-existing logical order, as a disordering in a scheme of classification. This transgression is interesting only because it creates meaning; as it is put in the Rhetoric [by Aristotle], metaphor "conveys learning and knowledge through the medium of the genus" (1410 b 13). What is being suggested, then, is this: should we not say that metaphor destroys an order only to invent a new one; and that the category-mistake is nothing but the complement of a logic of discovery? . . . Pushing this thought to the limit, one must say that metaphor bears information because it "redescribes" reality. Thus, the category-mistake is the de-constructive intermediary phase between description and redescription.[37]

This act of redescription, for Ricoeur, speaks to the power of the biblical narrative. He writes, "The paradoxical universe of the sacred, we said, is internally 'bound.' The paradoxical universe of the parable, the proverb, and the eschatological saying, on the contrary, is a 'burst' or an 'exploded' universe."[38]

Ricoeur addresses the historical development of secularity as a move from a mythical or enchanted world into a scientific and rational one. He discusses how the sacred is no longer objectively found in the world, as it was in former historical epochs. This leads him to ask important questions about the sacred in relation to the world, and whether humanity can live without it. He describes the iconoclastic movement of the Enlightenment, and takes this development as a given—realizing there is no going back. Yet, he makes the argument that cosmic symbolism that once revealed the sacred in the world did not die, but has been "transformed in passing from the realm of the sacred to that of proclamation."[39] Thus it is in proclamation of the word that the world is "redescribed"; the old order is ruptured by the poetic and mythic gospel and the identity of creation and humanity is given new meaning and a new future.

---

37. Ricoeur, *Rule of Metaphor*, 22.
38. Ricoeur and Wallace, *Figuring the Sacred*, 60.
39. Ibid., 66.

Ricoeur's schema of the power of poetic language establishes the dialectic of iconoclasm as the rupturing of the old order, and new creation as the redescription of the world. This, I believe, is the same dialectic found in Bonhoeffer's articulation of "religionless Christianity." The iconoclastic rupture of religious and ethical abstraction creates space for the revelation of God in Jesus Christ as the proclamation about the identity of God, humanity, creation, and the opening of the future. Thus, "religionless Christianity," as a process of "demythologization," gives way to the proclamation of Jesus Christ as the "center" of created life through a process of "remythologization." Bonhoeffer is not calling for the Christian community to accommodate itself to the presuppositions of the secularized and disenchanted world; he is calling the community to reclaim the poetic and mythological power of the gospel that redescribes the world and the identity of humanity in the context of the death and resurrection of Jesus Christ.

This dialectic of iconoclasm and redescription is the fundamental task of the Christian community as it addresses the lived experience of young people in the West. As the social imaginaries of young people have been formed and shaped by the economic function of secularity, the lives of young people are increasingly fragmented and abstracted. They are alienated from their embodied existence as the diverse complexity of their humanity is reduced to an economic function. Given the commodification of young people previously discussed, it is essential that youth ministry take up the movements of iconoclasm and redescription. This means proclaiming the word about Jesus Christ into the lives of young people through the use of "limit-expressions that bring about the rupturing of ordinary speech."[40] The economic and technological discourse at work in the lives of young people needs to be challenged, and the world of young people, including their humanity, needs to be redescribed so that they might embrace their humanity in response to the call of God heard and seen in Jesus Christ. This hermeneutical task provides the context for the Christian community to engage the lives of young people by taking seriously the significant cultural issues relating to faith and identity.

The Function of Popular Culture

An important aspect of this "remythologizing" hermeneutic is that the Christian community must take the cultural world of young people

40. Ibid., 60.

seriously. While global technocapitalism functions as the status quo, working to effectively homogenize and control the cultural world young people inhabit, it is important to acknowledge the subversive role of certain expressions of popular culture in the West. It is easy for the Christian community to dismiss popular culture as either a form of distraction or exploitation; however, it is important for the community to recognize the authentic attempts to articulate a love and passion for this life in the face of cultural forces that objectify and control.

The power of certain forms of popular culture such as music, film, television, etc. is found in their symbolic capacity. Different forms of music allow for the world to be described in the poetic or metaphorical using language and symbols. The significance of this form of expression is that the poetic does not attempt to control or objectify reality; instead, the poetic is a way to encounter and know the world differently. It is the poetic power of popular culture that has the potential to create space within the cultural experience of young people in which they are free to wrestle with questions of meaning and identity. At the same time, the poetic allows young people the opportunity to encounter transcendence without attempting to make it conform to human rationality.

The importance of popular culture for young people is that it represents an opportunity for them to assert agency and subjectivity within the context of the broader paradigm of global technocapitalism. It provides young people with the space to reconfigure and repackage what is given to them by technocapitalism as they employ popular tactics over and against the strategies of the dominant cultural forces that objectify human existence. Catholic sociologist Michel de Certeau understood the subversive potential of popular culture as an artistic endeavor that cultivates new ways of speaking (language), poetic ways of knowing (tales and legends), and "arts of practice" that divert time, establishing a subversive space within the context of the homogenized space of global technocapitalism.[41] Speaking of the subversive power of stories, he writes:

> The formality of everyday practices is indicated in these tales, which frequently reverse the relationships of power and, like the stories of miracles, ensure the victory of the unfortunate in a fabulous utopian space. This space protects the weapons of the weak against the reality of the established order. It also hides them from the social categories which "make history" because they dominate

41. Certeau, *Practice of Everyday Life*, 23.

it. And whereas historiography recounts in the past tense the strategies of instituted powers, these fabulous stories offer their audience a repertory of tactics for future use.[42]

Through these "tactics" individuals and communities are able to use the products produced by global technocapitalist against the system, what Certeau refers to as the process of "'putting one over' on the established order on its home ground."[43] This, for Certeau, is the significance of "popular culture," as it provides the context for subversive resistance to the strategic power of global capitalism—the possibility of making space, through artistic subversion, that is outside of the panoptic gaze. He writes:

> The actual order of things is precisely what "popular" tactics turn to their own ends, without any illusion that it will change any time soon. Though elsewhere it is exploited by a dominant power or simply denied by an ideological discourse, here order is tricked by an art. Into the institution to be served are thus insinuated styles of social exchange, technical invention, and moral resistance, that is, an economy of the "gift" (generosities for which one expects a return), an esthetics of "tricks" (artists' operations) and an ethics of tenacity (countless ways of refusing to accord the established order the status of law, a meaning, or a fatality). "Popular" culture is precisely that . . .[44]

While Bonhoeffer does not specifically address this issue in detail, there is much evidence that he was deeply influenced by significant manifestations of popular culture. During his time as a student at Union in the early 1930s Bonhoeffer was profoundly impacted by his experience of the Harlem Renaissance. Not only did this experience affect his theology by opening him to issues of race and social justice, but Bonhoeffer was also influenced by African American music, art, and worship. Scott Holland, in his essay "First We Take Manhattan, Then We Take Berlin: Bonhoeffer's New York," describes Bonhoeffer's interest in the music of Harlem and how this influenced his theology. He writes:

> Frank Fisher introduced Bonhoeffer to both sacred and secular Harlem, not that the two could always be easily pried apart. As a pastor, Bonhoeffer spoke of the Black church with uncharacteristic feeling. As a classical pianist, Bonhoeffer was very interested

42. Ibid.
43. Ibid., 26.
44. Ibid.

in the music. He found it strange and other yet he was fascinated by it. At Harlem, it seems, Bonhoeffer began to learn about the improvisation of jazz, the contingency of the blues, and the liberation of black spirituals. Much later in his intellectual and spiritual development he applied a musical rather than a biblical or ethical metaphor to the task of theology: polyphony. Theology, Bonhoeffer suggested, is neither a neat harmony nor a mere symphony, but it is a polyphony. A polyphony in this context is a musical piece in which two or more different melodies come together in a satisfying way. According to Bonhoeffer, the church's *cantus firmus*, its fixed traditional melody, must remain in place yet invite the addition and innovation of other voices into the flow of the music. The introduction of this metaphor into his theology marked a movement in his thought from the imitation motif of *The Cost of Discipleship* or *Nachfolge* to the more improvisational style of his later works, such as *Ethics* and *Letters and Papers from Prison*.[45]

Bonhoeffer's use of the term "polyphony" to describe life connects to his opposition to idealist abstraction. There can be no reduction of life to abstract principles, whether they are religious, moral, or economic. Christ, as the cantus firmus, the fixed center or melody, brings forth a polyphonic life that cannot be abstracted or objectified. The experience of this temporal life, the joys and sorrows, the "happiness and dange,r" is, for Bonhoeffer, "better than when one is to some degree cut off from the breath of life."[46] Thus, we find in Bonhoeffer's "religionless Christianity" the foundation for a poetic approach to life, one that takes the experiences of temporal life seriously by refusing to objectify them or reify them into abstract principles.

This is the significance of popular culture for young people living within the homogenizing idealism of technocapitalism. It represents a poetic critique of the domination of young people by the social and cultural forces of the status quo. It is the means by which the humanity of young people pushes back against the sinful distortion and objectifying spirit of contemporary Western culture. This is not to say that these forms of popular culture are capable of objectively revealing God or humanity, for to go this far is to fall into one more form of idealist objectification of transcendence. It is also important to acknowledge the sinful, objectifying tendencies that exist within these manifestations of popular culture. However, they do provide an essential dialogue partner for the Christian

---

45. Holland, "First We Take Manhattan."
46. *DBWE* 8:305.

community as it engages the lives of young people. There can be no love for young people, there can be no call to ethical responsibility, and there can be no humanization of young people without taking popular culture seriously.

The response of the Christian community to the current crisis of young people, faith, and the church must be informed by a theological understanding of faith, church, and the primary task of the Christian community in and for the world. Bonhoeffer's "religionless Christianity," in the context of his broader theological work, provides an important paradigm by which the community can address this issue. Bonhoeffer's theology helps the Christian community define faith, not as something that is produced, grown, or controlled, but as a way of knowing the revelation of God in the crucified and risen Christ. Jesus Christ is the object of faith for the Christian community, for in Jesus Christ humanity knows God and knows what it means to be a human being. In Jesus Christ the community knows of the restoration of the communion between God and humanity, and ultimately God and the world, a revelation that brings forth the actualization of the new humanity in the world: the church.

In all of this the Christian community comes to recognize that its primary task is not about self-preservation—it is a mission of love for the neighbor and for the world. The task of the church is humanization: proclaiming the new humanity revealed in Jesus Christ. This is a call to ethical responsibility for our neighbor, and it is a call to possess the courage and strength to embrace this finite, temporal human life as the life God has embraced and loves in Jesus Christ. The task of the church is to confront every attempt to dehumanize and objectify the lives of young people, which means the call of the church is to proclaim the death and resurrection of Jesus Christ as the affirmation of a polyphonic life over and against the commodifying power of global technocapitalism.

All of this leads to the question: What are the practical implications of religionless Christianity for the Christian community and youth ministry in particular? The final chapter will suggest guidelines for strategic action steps that engage the issue of young people, faith, and the Christian community.

Chapter 7

Conclusion

Poetic Youth Ministry

It's not often that one of the most powerful scenes in a film is the final credits, but this is certainly the case with *WALL-E*. As the film ends and Peter Gabriel begins to sing "Down to Earth," cartoon hieroglyphics show what life in a post-Axiom world looks like. The scenes show humans renewing and repopulating the earth, reconstructing houses and cultural spaces, and relearning how to farm and fish, all as vital parts of reclaiming an earthly life. The robots and technology haven't disappeared; they are repurposed as tools to help cultivate a new way of life. The final scene shows a picture of WALL-E and EVE standing in a field underneath a large tree. As the scene pans down we realize that this tree is the boot plant—the boot is planted in the earth among the roots digging deep into the ground.

These vignettes drive home the message of the film: human life is supposed to be a life lived in relationship with the earth. The frailty and vulnerability of an earthly life is not something to be overcome; it is what makes human life worth living. This is the same message young people need to hear from the Christian community as they live within the consumer society of Western culture. In the face of powerful technological, economic, and institutional voices calling young people to overcome their humanity, and to constantly recreate their identity, young people need to hear the good news about the way of life revealed in Jesus Christ that affirms their imperfect humanity and life lived in this world.

Young people are leaving the church. The response of the Christian community to this issue has been to focus on new forms of belief and practice grounded in a strong theology. There has also been an emphasis on adapting the beliefs and practices of the community to the new cultural changes that have occurred over the last fifty years. While these responses are well intended and raise important points that need to be considered, they fail to seriously engage the formative power of the broader social and cultural ideology of global technocapitalism and the consumer society.

An exploration of the contemporary Western cultural situation reveals a significant shift in "social imaginary" that influences the way young people in the West frame "objective reality." The consequence of this shift is that many people in the West increasingly struggle to find the Christian world view believable, let alone practical or useful. Instead, as their imaginations are increasingly shaped by the global technocapitalist ideology of the consumer society, a new form of religious belief has become prevalent within Western culture, a religious world view that Christian Smith has named "Moral Therapeutic Deism."

The question facing the Christian community is exactly how to respond to this new situation. One posture is to fall back into a form of sectarian fundamentalism and continue to believe the Christian world view in spite of scientific or economic changes. To do this risks establishing a form of dualism in which God is reduced to the personal or spiritual realm, apart from the cultural world. A second posture is to accommodate the Christian tradition to the principles of the broader cultural paradigm. As discussed above, both of these approaches are problematic because they fail to address the ideological nature of the broader social and cultural world of young people.

In the examples discussed above (*Almost Christian, You Lost Me, Sticky Faith, Jesus-Centered Youth Ministry,* etc.) much of the emphasis is placed on the development of processes to help young people remain faithful to the tradition as they live within Western culture. However, these projects fail to provide a thick description of what they mean by faith and discipleship. As these processes and practices become markers for the Christian community to determine whether young people have "faith," they risk being co-opted by the processes and techniques of global technocapitalism that shape young people to be part of the consumer society. The result is a never-ending cycle of desire by which young people commodify and recommodify themselves to make themselves desirable and consumable.

— CONCLUSION —

Unfortunately, by overemphasizing the process of faith the Christian community ends up unintentionally contributing to this cycle, entrenching Moral Therapeutic Deism as the default religious expression of young people in the West.

For the Christian community to take on Moral Therapeutic Deism it must first take seriously the experience of young people living under the formative influence of global technocapitalism and the consumer society. As demonstrated in the work of Zygmunt Bauman and Henry Giroux, the lives of young people are under the constant threat of commodification. They are constantly being abstracted and monetized through educational and social institutions that focus upon employment and economic productivity. Increasingly, the "success" or "failure" of young people is related to how well they are able to make themselves desirable to those who inhabit the networks of cultural power.

The Christian community needs to recognize that the issue of young people leaving the church is fundamentally a conflict of social imaginary; the beliefs and practice of the Christian community increasingly do not resonate with the lived reality of young people. Thus, young people are exchanging what they consider to be an outmoded social imaginary for one that is more relevant and practical. To put it another way, young people are exchanging the salvation offered by traditional forms of Christianity for the of salvation offered by the religious function of the consumer society.

The response of the Christian community must not focus on anxious attempts to control; instead, the community must practice a weakening form of love that challenges every religious and cultural power that tries to abstract and commodify the identity of young people by living as a sign of the new humanity of Jesus Christ. To put it simply, the church must be willing to let young people go, inviting them into a way of life that is grounded in love and grace, calling them to embrace their human identity in the new humanity of Jesus Christ. This is fundamentally a hermeneutical task, as the identity and cultural world of young people is redescribed by the death and resurrection of Jesus Christ.

All of this provides the context for a "poetic" form of youth ministry. "Poetic," in this context, refers to the playfulness of language and metaphor, a way of speaking that holds the world lightly. "Poetic youth ministry" is a form of youth ministry that seeks to humanize young people by holding them lightly in the face of the abstracting and objectifying forces of global technocapitalism. It is a form of pastoral ministry that attempts to redescribe or renarrate the world according to the gospel by entering into their lived experience and taking seriously the ethical responsibility to be with and for young people.[1] It is a form of ministry that does not fall back upon processes to mark or measure faith, but works to create space for young people to encounter the crucified and risen Christ. It is also a ministry of the Christian community that seeks to humanize young people by calling them to become ethically responsible for their humanity and the humanity of their neighbor. It is a ministry that is grounded in love.

The hermeneutical nature of "poetic youth ministry" means that the task of the youth pastor or youth leader is to be an "interpretive guide." In *An Introduction to Pastoral Care*, Charles Gerkin describes it this way:

> The role of pastoral leadership must more clearly and intentionally than in the recent past develop a quality of interpretive guidance. By interpretive guidance I mean not simply the interpretation of the Christian tradition and its implications for communal, moral, individual, and societal life, important as that is for the role of pastoral leadership and relational practice. I mean also the role of interpreting the conflicts and pressures, the contradictions and pitfalls, the lures and tendencies toward fragmentation of contemporary life. In short, I mean the role of interpretive guidance as it relates to facilitating the dialogical process between life stories and the Christian story of how life is to be lived.[2]

An essential part of this task is the role of the poetic in the formation and construction of identity. Gerkin emphasizes a cultural–linguistic approach to the task of pastoral care in which narrative functions to mediate the Christian tradition and the particular lives of young people. To use the concepts of Ricoeur, this takes place within the dialectic of "narration" and "renarration." Thus, the stories and symbols of the tradition are brought into dialogue with the particular stories and symbols that inform the identities of young people. While it is important to recognize the diversity of human experience, and thus the diversity of narratives present in the particular lives of young people, it is just as crucial that the broader social and cultural narrative of global technocapitalism, which undergirds the particular narratives of young people in the West, be taken into account.

---

1. For examples of practitioners and scholars within the field of youth ministry who take a similar approach, see Arthur, *God-Hungry Imagination*, and Turpin, *Branded*.

2. Gerkin, *Introduction to Pastoral Care*, 114.

—Conclusion—

The task of the youth pastor, as the representative of the community, is to provide a context in which the narratives that form the identity of young people (technocapitalism) are ruptured by the poetic limit language of the gospel. Through the proclamation of the gospel young people are confronted with the crucified and resurrected Christ mediated through the proclamation of the word, the celebration of the sacraments, and the practice of loving our neighbor. The social nature of youth ministry, which is symbolized in the relationship between the youth pastor, young people, the adults of the community, and the broader community (the world), means that these relationships become the place of encounter with the crucified and risen Christ.

This encounter functions as the "limit expression" that ruptures the stories that narrate the lives of young people, helping them to "renarrate" their identity in the context of the revelation of Jesus Christ, creating the space in which the Holy Spirit establishes the conditions for faith in which the love of God for the world is revealed.

At the same time, the lived experience of young people expressed in their cultural and social narratives pushes back against the religious and dogmatic categories of the tradition. Just as "poetic youth ministry" challenges the cultural forms of reification at work in the lives of young people, so too must it address the abstractions and reifications that occur within the Christian community. This is where the dialectic of "demythologization" and "remythologization" takes place, as the youth pastor brings the cultural issues and narratives of young people into dialogue with the tradition.[3] Just as the crucifixion and resurrection negate and recreate cultural identity, so too the symbols and stories that make up the tradition must not become absolute principles or strong doctrines. Instead, the symbols and stories must be held loosely as they are interpreted and reinterpreted in relation to the experiences of young people. The task of youth ministry is to provide young people with a poetic articulation of the Christian tradition that guards against every form of religious abstraction that Bonhoeffer opposed.

This poetic hermeneutic allows the gospel to rupture and renarrate the identity and lived experience of young people in the context of the new humanity revealed in Jesus Christ. This approach allows the Christian

---

3. Serene Jones frames justification and sanctification in a similar way, suggesting that justification represents a deconstruction of identity while sanctification speaks to human identity being reconstituted. See her *Feminist Theory and Christian Theology*.

community to engage young people without coercion or indoctrination. While it is important for the church to claim a particular doctrinal and confessional identity, providing the foundation for communion and dialogue with other traditions, it must do this poetically in a way that grounds the life of the community in grace and love. In all of this the community demonstrates that the purpose of Christian faith is not to keep people in the church, but that the purpose of Christian faith is a way of life that becomes a living sign of the grace and love of God for the world in Jesus Christ.

Poetic Youth Ministry: What Does It Look Like?

To give a prescriptive response to the problem of young people leaving the church would contradict much of what I have argued about weak theology and a posture of love. It is the responsibility of each community to engage young people within the historical and cultural world they inhabit, which means it is the responsibility of each community to work out the pragmatic details that address its own context. However, there are some general guidelines that can provide a picture of what a poetic form of youth ministry might look like.

Poetic Youth Ministry: Encounter Rather Than Growth

One of the consequences of consumer society is that the principles of growth, progress, and measurement are increasingly inscribed into the objective reality of young people. The institutional world they inhabit constantly measures, assesses, and grades them, prompting them to constantly improve. The world of young people has quickly become a world of performance, where they are asked to meet the expectations and requirements of adults and institutions. They are constantly held up to abstracted forms of the ideal human: ideal student, ideal athlete, ideal musician, ideal employee, etc. This pervasive assessment establishes the boundary lines for what is considered "normal," which are then used to label and categorize the lives of young people. Success and failure are measurements to determine the degree to which they have attained this ideal, determining whether they become what Bauman describes as either a "successful" or the "failed commodity."

A religious approach to youth ministry emphasizes abstract standards that define what it means to be an "ideal" member of the community. In

—Conclusion—

this context, piety, morality, and doctrinal belief become the standards by which young people are assessed. These abstract ideals also become the means by which various forms and practices in youth ministry are determined to be successful. Often, those who meet these expectations are held up to be the examples, or they are given positions of leadership, reaffirming the message of inclusion or exclusion based on how well they live into moral and doctrinal ideals. At the same time, dominant social and cultural ideals increasingly determine the standards by which young people are judged to be successful. Here, the cultural discourses that establish what is considered "normal" play out within the Christian community as the ideals that are deemed desirable (beauty, athleticism, academic success, artistic ability, etc.) become indicators of faith and leadership.

A "poetic" approach to youth ministry works to create a space in which young people can step out of these cultural and social expectations and get out from under these labels and expectations. Rather than establish one more set of expectations to which young people must adhere (piety, morality, or doctrinal belief), poetic youth ministry seeks to create a space in which young people can begin to narrate their human identity as they encounter Jesus Christ in their peers and the adults within the community. This means creating a space in which young people are exposed to the finite, creaturely nature of their humanity in a way that shows there is no "ideal" humanity; there are only real human beings who exist in relationship with each other. Thus, the purpose of poetic youth ministry is to establish a counternarrative to the technocapitalist paradigm that is grounded in the death and resurrection of Jesus Christ, allowing them to embrace their finite humanity.

Essential to this form of youth ministry is moving away from the language of "building" and "progress." A person does not become more or less Christian, just as a person does not become more or less human; there is only difference. To live as a human necessarily means that we change; however, we must be careful how this change is labeled and identified so we don't fall into the idealist trap of objectification. A deeper understanding of piety, morality, or doctrinal belief represent significant change within the experience of a young person, but this does not necessarily mean a person has "more" or "less" faith. Youth ministry should not make piety, morality, or doctrinal belief the markers of faith; instead, youth ministry must focus upon creating space for young people to encounter God and their own humanity revealed in Jesus Christ.

Poetic Youth Ministry

The purpose of youth ministry is not to help young people "grow" or "develop" into better or more spiritual Christians; the focus of pastoral youth ministry is to help young people continually renarrate their lives and their relationship to the world in relation to the story of Jesus. The biblical story does not function as a manual of spiritual growth or a deposit of absolute truths to be memorized and internalized; instead, the biblical story functions as a powerful counternarrative to the narratives and discourses of consumer society. This approach allows youth ministry to provide a biblical approach to the interpretive pastoral task that untangles or differentiates the humanity of young people from the names and labels given to young people through the normalizing processes of the consumer society.[4]

One way youth ministry and pastoral care can help young people think about this renarration of identity is by practicing a form of externalization. In narrative therapy "externalizing the problem" is an interpretive process that allows individuals to separate an issue or problem from their core identity. An important part of this process is to name the dominant cultural narratives that are given power and authority. This power derives from the way these stories are internalized, which means they shape the social imagination in such a way that they become "normalized" objective reality. To externalize the problem is to give voice to other narratives—other ways of seeing the world—that challenge or question this new "normalized" reality. Through this process the identity of the individual person is differentiated from the dominant discourse, opening up new possibilities for agency and the renarration of identity. Michael White, in *Narrative Means to Therapeutic Ends*, describes it this way: "The externalization of the problem enables persons to separate from the dominant stories that have been shaping their lives and relationships. In so doing, persons are able to identify previously neglected but vital aspects of lived experience—aspects that could not have been predicted from a reading of the dominant story. Thus . . . I have referred to these aspects of experience as 'unique outcomes.'"[5]

---

4. See White and Epston, *Narrative Means*. White writes, "'Externalizing' is an approach to therapy that encourages persons to objectify and, at times, to personify the problems that they experience as oppressive. In this process, the problem becomes a separate entity and thus external to the person or relationship that was ascribed as the problem. Those problems that are considered to be inherent, as well as those relatively fixed qualities that are attributed to persons and to relationships, are rendered less fixed and less restricting." Ibid., 38.

5. Ibid., 41.

—Conclusion—

In response to the problem of young people leaving the church, youth ministry can begin to reclaim the biblical narrative from the fundamentalist and liberal trappings by allowing the narrative of Scripture to become a rupturing and externalizing force over and against the dominant global technocapitalist narrative and consumer society. Youth ministry, in this context, becomes a crucial space in which young people construct what White refers to as "alternative stories" or "unique accounts" of their identities. Through the cultivation of a biblical and prophetic imagination the practices of youth ministry can help young people reimagine their identity and their relationship to the world.

The task of youth pastors and youth leaders is to help create space in which young people are able to imagine what it means to live as the new humanity in Jesus Christ. This means creating a form of ministry that is willing to challenge the dominant cultural narratives by opening up space for dialogue. Rather than establishing a new objectifying discourse of rigid biblical or moral principles, or by trying to accommodate Christian belief to the dominant cultural paradigm, youth ministry must be a place that helps young people learn how to ask questions. This is where the biblical story functions as a disruptive force, clearing the space for important questions and alternative stories that point to our human identity grounded in Jesus Christ.

This approach points to the theological and pastoral function of the Christian community in how it ministers to young people. It affirms the role of youth pastor as interpretive guide as she or he interprets and reinterprets both the lived experience of young people and the biblical and theological narratives. The task of the youth pastor is to develop the ability to read both the cultural and social experiences of young people in dialogue with the biblical and theological tradition—holding both loosely in order to prevent the objectification of the Bible or the dominant cultural narratives. Through the rupture of the biblical narrative, and the dialectic of narration and renarration, young people are opened to the possibility of divine encounter (Jesus Christ) by the power and work of the Holy Spirit.

A few years back I was asked to speak at a youth convention. I began with a clip from the first Harry Potter film, *Harry Potter and the Sorcerer's Stone*, in which Harry is barricaded in a house by his aunt and uncle—the Dursleys.[6] A knock at the door reveals a large, burly man named Hagrid, who informs Harry that he is in fact a wizard. The power of this narrative is

---

6. Columbus, *Sorcerer's Stone*.

that it focuses upon a young boy who has been told all of his life that there is nothing good or special about him. Hagrid literally breaks into Harry's life and speaks a new, powerful word that reveals to him there is much more to his identity: he is a wizard.

Following this clip I asked the young people to help me make a list of all of the stories and narratives at work in their lives. At first the room was silent, but one by one they began to speak up. By the end the white board was full of the names and stories given to them by their social and cultural world. They listed traits like "ugly," "overweight," "stupid," and "outcast," but they also listed the expectations their social communities pressed upon them to be "athletic," "smart," and "successful." They also spoke about the pressure to be "religious," "moral," and "good." We spent some time exploring where these ideals come from and how they are all grounded in specific narratives or discourses that determine what is "normal." My purpose was to help them see that, like Harry Potter, they take on (internalize) the "names" and expectations of the social and cultural narratives at work in their lives.

From this discussion we moved on to talk about the gospel, specifically focusing on how Paul describes how we have been given a new name in Jesus Christ. The point of this discussion was to name and externalize the stories at work in the lives of young people in order to create space for them to begin to renarrate their identity in the context of the gospel.

Poetic Youth Ministry Affirms the Humanity of Young People

As discussed above, the problem with consumer society is that it works to fragment and abstract the humanity of young people by prompting them to overcome their finite, temporal, human nature. The objectification and commodification of young people within this new cultural situation can lead to an ethical approach in which everything is reduced to a means to an end. Ethical decisions become grounded in idealist notions of the higher good in which concrete existential decisions are sacrificed for the sake of ideal principles.

For Bonhoeffer this can be seen in various forms of religion where finite, temporal life is viewed as less important than "eternal" principles. In the name of holiness, piety, or some eternalized view of heaven, the creaturely humanity of young people is reduced to "glorifying God" or "getting to heaven." Love for the neighbor is also framed in the terms of principles

—Conclusion—

or ideals that make the concrete reality of the neighbor secondary to this higher good. The popular cliché "love the sinner and hate the sin" promotes a form of detached service that prevents the community from becoming fully immersed in the experience of the neighbor. The neighbor becomes an abstraction as the part that is worthy of love, the spiritual, is separated from the part that is broken and sinful, the finite and temporal. In this context, "loving our neighbor" becomes a way for young people to live up to the expectations of the adult community by demonstrating their faith, even if it ends up dehumanizing the neighbor by sublimating her or him to the principles of a higher good. In all of this the new humanity of Jesus Christ is kept from touching the concrete experiences of young people.

In response to the pragmatic abstraction of technocapitalism and the consumer society, poetic youth ministry affirms the goodness of embodied, temporal life. One important way in which it can do this is by fostering an environment of "play." A youth ministry that takes seriously the theological significance of play establishes the conditions for a significant counternarrative to the discourse of technocapitalism. For the pragmatic, mechanical world of technocapitalism, play is pointless. There is no higher purpose or meaning that play seeks to attain; it represents the engagement of an activity for its own sake. Stuart Brown, who has studied and written extensively on the biological and psychological benefits of play, argues that play is purposeless because it lacks "survival value." He writes, "They don't help in getting food. They are not done for their practical value. Play is done for its own sake."[7] Jürgen Moltmann offers a similar theological interpretation. He writes, "It is only in play that human beings can endure the fundamental contingency of the world and adapt to that contingency. In play human beings display and maintain their own liberty. In play they weigh up the chances of a fortuitous world and the forces of their own freedom. The kingdom of freedom is the kingdom of play . . . Meaningful but not necessary: this is what characterizes play compared with purposeful and utilitarian work."[8]

Play represents a diminishment of consciousness that unifies the ego, and its ability for self-reflection, with the body and action. As individuals lose themselves in play they stop thinking or worrying about social perceptions as they get caught up in the event. This sense of playfulness is an opportunity for young people to break free from the narratives and

7. Brown and Vaughan, *Play*, 17.
8. Moltmann, *God in Creation*, 310–11.

requirements of the dominant cultural paradigm while creating a space in which the finite human experience of young people is affirmed. In breaking free from the conscious awareness of the internalized standards of what constitutes "normal" or "successful," young people are free to experience the limits of their humanity as they are caught up into the exhilaration of losing oneself in activity for its own sake. These experiences allow young people to test their limits, to risk, to fail, and ultimately to experience a form of joy that is grounded in the finite, temporal human existence.

Youth ministry has tried to become more serious over the last decade by working to overcome the stereotype that it is all about games and food. Yet, when placed within a proper theological framework, playing and eating together is increasingly what young people need. Reclaiming a sense of playfulness can be an important way for youth ministry to provide a counternarrative to the fragmented, hyperpragmatic consumer culture by providing young people with an opportunity to lose themselves in activity, and to become open to the concrete, embodied nature of their own identity and the identity of the other.

An example of this is the work of a pastor who led a junior high and high school group at a church in an urban area. Young people from the neighborhood were invited to come be a part of what by all appearances was a typical youth ministry program. The night began with some sort of activity, usually in the form of competitive games. However, the pastor always picked games that required a different skill set than the ones used in the major team sports like football, volleyball, or basketball. Most of the young people had never played them before, which resulted in most of them doing poorly. Usually, there were one or two young people who were not successful athletes who ended up doing very well. The intended result of these activities was to place young people in a position of failure, to have them become vulnerable to their peers through their awkward participation in a game at which they were not very good, and to allow others, who normally were not celebrated for their athletic skill, to experience success.

From the outside this pastor's ministry looked like a typical youth ministry with quirky, eccentric games. However, this pastor intentionally focused on creating a space where young people could lose themselves in a form of play that brought their finite human abilities to the forefront in a positive way. These games were one small attempt to provide a counterexperience to the broader cultural fear of failure, and the desire to overcome the finite, vulnerable nature of our humanity. In doing so, they provided important glimpses of the new humanity of Jesus Christ made present within the Christian community that affirm the goodness of finite human experience.

Poetic Youth Ministry Fosters the Courage to Be Human

Closely related to the humanization of young people in youth ministry is an approach that cultivates the courage and strength to embrace human life with all of its joy, happiness, grief, and struggle. This means equipping young people to live as humans within the reality of this world by refusing to appeal to abstract principles as the higher purpose or meaning for this life. Young people must be encouraged to embrace the significance of this life with all of its joys and sorrows, and to have the courage and strength to engage the significant issues that confront their human experience. The task of poetic youth ministry is to help young people negotiate the significant issues and struggles they face in the adolescent stage of life, not according to some form of absolute truth, whether it is moral, doctrinal, or cultural, but according to the revelation of God and humanity in Jesus Christ. For this to happen youth ministry must be a place that intentionally establishes a space for difficult questions and issues to be explored.

The community must be willing to engage difficult topics in a way that encourages young people to develop a sense of responsibility for their peers, for their neighbors, and for the world. This means facilitating important conversations about issues such as sex, abortion, poverty, violence, and gender without resorting to answers grounded in absolute reified ideals. Youth ministry must foster open dialogue about issues of social justice in a way that avoids the pitfalls of political ideology while helping young people live into their responsibility for the other. This means having important conversations about relational issues, family issues, and the emotional struggles of anxiety and depression, and it means taking the hopes and fears of young people seriously by helping them narrate and renarrate the significance of work and vocation.

Young people must also be given the space to grieve and mourn in the face of death and suffering; they need the community to both model grief and provide the appropriate space in which they can experience the emotion and pain that is an important part of the human experience of love. Certainly, this process includes the Christian hope of resurrection and the future life. But this hope must not take away from the significance of this temporal life by referring to some "heavenly home" or "better place" when loved ones go when they die; it must affirm the meaning and significance of this life by taking seriously the grief and loss experienced in the death of a loved one.

Serene Jones speaks to this in her book *Trauma and Grace* by focusing upon the experience of trauma and the way in which it "reconfigures" the imagination and the narration of lived experience.[9] It is in the context of this rupture of imagination and narrative that youth ministry and the Christian community can help young people begin to renarrate their lives in the context of the gospel. Jones writes:

> This is a tall order, but we do not have to start from scratch. Christianity does not need to discern the relationships between trauma and grace from a blank slate; after all, it was founded on the story of the crucifixion and resurrection of Jesus. So in a very real way its central story is one of trauma and grace. In the same way, the church has struggled to speak to its believers for centuries—sometimes in successful ways, sometimes not so successfully. . . . The language of faith can reach straight into the heart of the imagination. The fragmented anatomy of trauma can leave one without a world, without speech, stories, memory, community, future, or a sense of self; theology's task is to re-narrate to us what we have yet to imagine.[10]

I recently spent time talking with a young woman who had a close friend die in an accident. As she talked about her loss, she struggled to find the language to express her feelings. She talked about how so many in the Christian community tried to comfort her with language of heaven as a "better place" and our "eternal home." I could tell that she struggled with this understanding of death.

After she finished speaking I told her about the loss my wife and I experienced. Our youngest daughter, Savannah, is a twin. We found out early in the pregnancy that one daughter would live and the other would die. When the girls were born we spent the day holding and loving our other daughter, Vanessa, until she died that evening. I told her that we had to endure well-intentioned people trying to comfort us with an eternalized, otherworldly heaven. We listened politely, and thanked them for their support. However, I shared with her that this is not what we believe. Our daughter, I told her, was meant to be here, with us. She was meant to run

---

9. Jones, *Trauma and Grace*, 20.
10. Ibid., 21.

—Conclusion—

and play, grow and develop, and experience the joys and sufferings of this life. We grieved her death, as we should have, because young babies are not supposed to die. However, I also shared with her our hope and belief that because of Christ's resurrection our daughter is not lost.

Her response was one of gratitude, not because she agreed with my understanding of death or heaven, but because she was given the space to grieve and to wish her loved one were still alive. This, I believe, is what Jones means by theology "renarrating" what we cannot yet articulate or imagine. And this is one of the fundamental tasks of poetic youth ministry.

Similarly, youth ministry must provide a place where young people can explore important questions and issues that pertain to embodied sexuality. Rather than appeal to abstract moral principles or to a mechanistic obsession with technique, the Christian community can become a place where young people safely explore what it means to be a sexual human person made in the image of God. Being responsible for young people in this context means acknowledging the differences and the unique experiences of young people with regard to sexuality. While these differences make this issue much more complicated, to take them seriously models for young people what it means to embrace sexuality as a healthy part of human identity.[11]

An important part of helping young people wrestle with issues of sexuality is the issue of gender—providing a space for them to wrestle with what it means to be male and female. Again, the community must avoid falling into stereotypes by refusing to give in to abstract cultural ideals and principles that are reified into biblical or theological truths. The community must work to challenge every reified understanding of gender identity so that young people can experience and encounter what it means to be female and male in the context of the new humanity revealed in Jesus Christ. This means addressing the difficult issues regarding biblical and theological articulations of gender, as well as providing a space for young people to

---

11. For an approach to discussing the issue of sex and sexuality, see Smedes, *Sex for Christians*. Smedes writes, "There are rules, to be sure. And any Christian will take them seriously. But what we need to find out is whether there is an insight, a vision, that tells us what the deeper significance of sexuality and sexual behavior is. . . . To locate the real message of the Bible concerning sexuality, we will have to see how our sexuality and our sexual living is embraced within the gospel. If we can manage that, we will be in a position to discern the limits implicit in the liberty—and the liberty within the limits—of our sexual life in Christ." Ibid., 12.

critically examine the cultural paradigms that inform how they understand their own gender.

One way to approach this issue that offers insight for youth pastors and those involved in the pastoral care of young people is the narrative approach described by Christine Neuger in *Counseling Women: A Narrative Pastoral Approach*. Neuger emphasizes the importance of unmasking the pervasive power of patriarchy within the dominant social and cultural structures. She describes how the dominant narrative of patriarchy inscribes not only the "norms" and "truths" regarding what it means to be a woman, but it also inscribes correlating "norms" regarding the nature of masculine identity. Neuger discusses the five-phase form of "gender training" that initiates young people into cultural articulations of gender that are based in patriarchal dominance and power. Through the five phases of humiliation, inculcation, retribution, conversion, and conscription, women learn a particular narrative and language of gender that is inscribed within their identity.[12] Neuger insists that a counselor must beware of the powerful ideological narratives at work in the lives of men and women. To this I would add that those involved in the task of youth ministry must also become aware of these powerful ideological narratives. Neuger writes, "It is the responsibility of counselors [youth pastors] to have a complex enough understanding of the cultural dynamics around sexism, racism, classism, and heterosexism that they can place the particular stories of counselees [young people] in the context of those dynamics. In doing pastoral counseling, the pastoral counselor must know about the cultural realities for women and men, of all races and classes, that, if unknown, distort the counselees' stories in harmful ways."[13]

In response to this situation Neuger advocates for narrative-based pastoral counseling that externalizes the problem of patriarchy and gives voice to the language and stories that have been "denied, minimized, and

---

12. Neuger, *Counseling Women*, 46–48. Neuger describes a five-phase form of gender training. Humiliation speaks to the "experience of being demeaned and devalued in one's own and others' eyes." Inculcation speaks to the phase when "girls and women are taught what it means to be female." Retribution is "the punishment for breaking the rules of being female." Conversion refers to the phase when women "learn to believe that who they have been named to be and the rules they have been taught are actually true and natural." Conscription is the "process of women attempting to persuade and convert other women to patriarchy's point of view about gender." Ibid.

13. Ibid., 15.

—CONCLUSION—

distorted by the dominant culture."[14] She writes, "The pastoral counselor and the counselee must work together to find the language that will authentically express the nature and power of the narrative. It is in finding the language and claiming the right to speak it that empowerment for change is made possible."[15]

Youth ministry can incorporate Neuger's insight in such a way that youth pastors and leaders proactively help young people renarrate their gendered and sexual identity within the context of the death and resurrection of Jesus Christ. Through the dialectic of narration and renarration, bringing into dialogue the biblical narrative, the social sciences, and cultural theory, youth leaders can help young people negotiate and reimagine what it means to be female and male in the context of the revelation of God in Jesus Christ. By demonstrating the problems with the strong doctrinal and dogmatic positions, as well as the cultural interpretations of gender, youth ministry can be a place where young people wrestle with important questions that pertain to gender and sexuality.

Similarly, poetic youth ministry should focus upon cultivating a thoughtful engagement of social justice issues. For many in youth ministry this means an emphasis upon service and mission projects as a way to put the gospel into practice by loving our neighbor. Such projects do provide a valuable cross-cultural experience for young people, placing them within diverse contexts with foreign social and cultural patterns. Yet, there is an implicit danger that the current emphasis upon mission projects leads to the dehumanization and the solidification of patterns of behaviors and mind-sets that are unhelpful at best and violent at worst. Youth pastors and leaders must work to poetically subvert the deeply ingrained narratives about race, gender, and cultural identity through important biblical and theological conversations about social and cultural issues. Youth pastors and leaders, as well as other members of the community, must do the careful work of preparing young people for mission trips and service projects so that the focus is upon the complexity of social problems and the diversity of human experience. In this context young people are encouraged to open themselves up to the "other" as they guard against every inclination to domesticate and objectify others according to our own social and cultural principles.[16]

14. Ibid., 71.
15. Ibid.
16. For further discussion of mission and service projects see Root's chapter, "The

One summer I was a part of a team that planned a high school service project that focused on rural communities in northwest Iowa and northeast Nebraska. Forty to fifty high school students, along with the leaders, stayed in a church in Sergeant Bluff, Iowa, working on the Winnebago Reservation and doing odd jobs for elderly widows. We framed the conversation in the terms of encountering God in our neighbor. The young people were encouraged to see their work not as charity or pity, but as an opportunity to meet and experience people from cultures and communities that were very different from their own. We asked them to reflect upon how God is at work in the world in the people they encountered, inviting them to step outside of the way they usually see the world, to experience it from the perspective of others. Overall, the week was very positive. Much work was done, but more importantly, each night young people gave their testimony, bearing witness to the different ways they saw God at work in lives of those they encountered.

Ultimately, to foster the courage to be human means, for Bonhoeffer, to help young people become responsible for their own humanity. This happens as they become responsible for the other as they encounter their neighbor and experience the world. For Bonhoeffer, this is only possible because of the revelation of God in Jesus Christ—the revelation of a way of life that doesn't need to appeal to some higher moral or religious abstraction for its meaning. The meaning of life is revealed through faith as young people encounter God and their humanity in Jesus Christ, an encounter that opens them to a way of being in the world that is grounded in love.

Poetic Youth Ministry: Charity over Doctrine and Piety

In emphasizing a poetic approach to the Christian tradition, youth ministry opposes reified and objectified expressions that create barriers of inclusion and exclusion based upon adherence or subscription to specific doctrinal and moral propositions. This is not to say that doctrine and dogma are insignificant. Rather, it is to emphasize a specific approach to doctrine and dogma that leave space for human life through interpretation and reinterpretation. Poetic youth ministry is not interested in burdening young people with abstract manifestations of absolute, unmediated truth; instead the emphasis is upon a playful dialectic of interpretation and reinterpretation within diverse historical and cultural contexts. In this way, Scripture,

---

Mission Trip as Global Tourism," in Root and Dean, *Theological Turn in Youth Ministry.*

—Conclusion—

doctrines, and confessions function less as repositories of absolute unmediated truth and more as poetic and metaphorical descriptions of the experience of God in Jesus Christ.

Similarly, morality and ethics should not be taught as absolute moral principles abstracted from the realities of cultural and social life; instead, morality and ethics should be seen as the responsibility to live as the new humanity in Jesus Christ within the historical and cultural reality of temporal life. While it might be easier to insist that young people adhere to abstract, absolute moral principles, to do so is to violate the humanity of young people as they are given the option of compromise in the name of some higher ideal. Thus, for Bonhoeffer, to focus upon absolute moral principles or a system of ethics is to open young people to the irresponsibility of abstraction. This means that they are given the option of adhering to a "higher" moral principle rather than taking responsibility for the neighbor they encounter.

Instead, youth ministry must take the time to do the hard work of helping young people become responsible for their neighbor, and in that encounter, to become responsible for their own decisions and actions as the new humanity in Jesus Christ. This is the foundation of morality and ethics: the concrete reality of human existence and decision as we encounter Jesus Christ through our neighbor. The Christian community is responsible to pastorally guide young people in a manner that teaches them through Scripture, tradition, and the confessions, but to do so in a way that invokes charity and love in responsibility for our neighbor. This, for Bonhoeffer, is what it means to be human in Jesus Christ.

A youth pastor once shared with me her experience of having a young man reveal that he was a homosexual. What complicated this experience is the community this young man lived in held to more conservative or traditional views of sexuality and marriage. While the people in this community would talk about needing to love homosexuals, they often used the language of "love the sinner, hate the sin." For this young man there was no struggle; he emphatically claimed to be a homosexual and a Christian, and he was ready to share this part of his identity with the broader community.

As this process unfolded the youth pastor became an advocate for this young man in multiple ways. She challenged members of her community to avoid falling back into principles and regulations, insisting that they recognize the young man not as some abstraction or problem to be dealt with, but a concrete human being. She acknowledged that many in the community held to certain interpretations of Scripture that made this situation difficult. The youth pastor pastorally encouraged the community to adhere to Paul's words in 1 Corinthians about love and charity, acknowledging the different perspectives, as she invited the community members, regardless of their beliefs, to practice the love that Paul advocates for the Christian community.

At the same time the youth pastor encouraged this young man to act out of love for the community, recognizing that some would have difficulty with the news, and that many would not know how to respond. Pastorally speaking, this youth leader became an advocate for this young man by helping him be honest about his sexuality without destroying the relationships he valued. While this was, and remains, a difficult process, overall this approach has been positive for both this young man and his Christian community.

I share this story as an example of how poetic youth ministry can be a crucial place in which youth pastors and youth leaders help young people and the Christian community guard against reducing human identity and experience to reified theological or doctrinal abstractions. Instead, youth ministry can become a place where young people embrace their concrete human identity in the context of the new humanity revealed in Jesus Christ.

Poetic Youth Ministry and the Lived Experience of Young People

As discussed above, the dialectic of "narration" and "renarration" involves a hermeneutical movement between the Christian tradition and the cultural narratives that influence the lives of young people. This should not be a movement in one direction (tradition to culture); it must be a dialogical movement, back and forth, from the cultural world of young people to the tradition and vice versa. This means that the various expressions of popular culture must be taken seriously, not just as something to be critiqued, but as serious manifestations of the agency and subjectivity of young people as they attempt to form and shape an identity. To take popular culture seriously is a messy and difficult endeavor, one that takes time, patience, and a willingness to seriously engage a variety of cultural expressions. This does not mean that youth pastors have to like or embrace everything in popular culture, but it does mean that they need to be able to speak the cultural language.

—Conclusion—

An important aspect of this interpretive dialogue is a critique of the symbols and narratives of popular culture by the tradition. There is an iconoclastic move from the tradition to popular culture that is necessary and important for helping young people renarrate their identity. However, it is important, as discussed above, to recognize the power and significance of the symbolic within popular culture, and the ways in which these symbols function to rupture the ideological power of the status quo. Here, the tradition must take seriously the power and message of these symbols, and youth ministry must make space for them within its teaching and practice.[17]

This is where popular culture provides a valuable critique of the tradition, forcing the community, and youth ministry, to interpret and reinterpret the tradition in the context of the cultural experience of young people. This occurs as the poetic and symbolic power of popular culture ruptures the status quo, creating space for the tradition to be reinterpreted as it encounters the lived experience of young people.

Practically, this means that popular culture must play a central role in the life of youth ministry. Youth leaders can use elements of popular culture to frame and discuss the experiences of young people, and youth leaders and/or teachers can use elements of popular culture in their teaching of Scripture and the confessions or doctrines. Popular culture can frame the conversations that address significant life experiences and issues young people are dealing with. It can also foster and solidify the social experience of the group through shared narratives and experiences that build community. Certain elements of popular culture also offer important entry points of conversation and connection with young people, both with those who are members of the community and more importantly with those who are not. While this engagement of popular culture adds a dimension of complexity and messiness to the task of youth ministry, it is an essential part of the hermeneutical task for the engagement of the lives of young people.

Finally, it is crucial that youth ministry become an opportunity for youth pastors, youth leaders, and members of the Christian community to become advocates for young people in the face of the dominant, fragmenting power of technocapitalism. Advocacy for youth in this context means equipping them with the necessary tools to negotiate and navigate the dominant cultural reality. In offering a critique of the lived experience of global technocapitalism it is important to acknowledge that it is the reality

---

17. See Lief, "Some Kind of Monstrosity." Also see Rose, *Hip Hop Wars*.

facing young people in the West. Thus, it is important that young people are able to develop the tools necessary to survive the technocapitalist world.

The Christian community can foster the humanity of young people by helping them cultivate these skills. This provides the context for congregations to establish programs that help young people develop these important skills. This includes academic skills such as reading, writing, and the ability to do math; financial skills like developing a budget, saving money, and balancing a checkbook or credit card statement; helping young people understand the function of credit and credit cards; or helping young people develop skills like cooking, carpentry, gardening, etc. Some communities can even develop tutoring programs and mentoring programs to help young people navigate the social and cultural landscape.

The purpose of this approach is not to accommodate the gospel to the technocapitalist paradigm but to equip young people with the skills and tools they need to engage the cultural realities of technocapitalism so they can be empowered to promote change. To use the language of sociologist Michel de Certeau, this approach creates the space for young people to engage in subversive tactics over and against the strategies of the status quo. Certeau writes, "The space of a tactic is the space of the other. Thus, it must play on and with a terrain imposed on it and organized by the law of a foreign power. It does not have the means to keep to itself, at a distance, in a position of withdrawal, foresight, and self collection: it is a maneuver 'within the enemy's field of vision' . . . and within enemy territory."[18]

Certeau discusses how people who are oppressed and disenfranchised are able to subvert the status quo by making "something else" out of what was provided to them by the dominant culture. He writes:

> [T]hey made something else out of them; they subverted them from within—not by rejecting them or by transforming them (though that occurred as well), but by many different ways of using them in the service of rules, customs or convictions foreign to the colonization which they could not escape. They metaphorized the dominant order: they made it function in another register. They remained other within the system which they assimilated and which assimilated them externally. They diverted it without leaving it. Procedures of consumption maintained their difference in the very space that the occupier was organizing.[19]

18. Certeau, *Practice of Everyday Life*, 37.
19. Ibid., 32.

—Conclusion—

This can and should be the function of youth ministry: to help young people name and externalize the dominant technocapitalist social imaginary, and to help them develop the tools necessary to navigate and survive within this paradigm so they can begin to renarrate the world according the revelation of God in Jesus Christ.

A concrete example of this is the Cristo Rey network of Catholic schools that started in Chicago and has developed in urban areas around the nation.[20] Cristo Rey Jesuit High School, in Minneapolis, works to equip young people from economically impoverished neighborhoods to be able to go to college, where they can develop the social capital necessary to navigate the technocapitalist paradigm. While students are required to learn about the Roman Catholic faith, the mission is not to convert or indoctrinate young people into Roman Catholic theology. The mission and purpose is to humanize young people by equipping them with the skills necessary to navigate Western culture. Ultimately, the hope is that young people will use these skills to promote social and political change on behalf of those who do not benefit from the economic, social, and political structures of the status quo.

In a similar way youth ministry can use the resources of the community to help young people negotiate the cultural world of technocapitalism. While this will most likely differ in scale from the Cristo Rey model, there are plenty of opportunities for churches and parachurch organizations to equip and empower young people to negotiate the cultural terrain in order to bring about cultural change and transformation.

Youth ministry also provides an opportunity for the Christian community to become advocates for young people within the context of consumer society. Because young people lack the political power of other groups, youth ministry can function in a way that calls adults to come alongside young people in times of difficulty. As young people face the pressures of school systems, employment, peer networks, and family situations, they need adults to support and advocate for them. This must not be interpreted as a form of soft love that does not hold young people responsible for their actions; instead, this is a vision of pastoral care that invites young people to become human by taking responsibility for their decisions and actions, giving valuable support and encouragement as young people engage the power and structures of the status quo.

---

20. See Kearney, *More Than a Dream*.

A concrete example of this comes from my time mentoring young people as a chaplain at Cristo Rey Jesuit High School in Minneapolis. I worked with a Muslim student who was at risk of losing his school-to-work job, which meant that he was in danger of being asked to leave the school. He had failed to complete certain tasks, for which he needed to take responsibility; however, there were also deeper cultural issues that needed to be addressed with regard to the place of employment. During a meeting I sat beside him as he faced questions from the adults sitting across the table. I spoke up in his defense, acknowledging his culpability, while arguing for a second chance in a new location that would be more sensitive to his Muslim identity. When the meeting was over, and the young man was given a second chance, he expressed much gratitude for the words of support, and it strengthened his trust in me as a mentor.

This is the type of responsibility youth pastors and leaders must take for the young people who are a part of the community. The focus is not to build large youth groups, or even to keep these young people in the church; the focus is to call them into their humanity by helping them take responsibility for the other, and live a life of charity and grace. By coming alongside young people and becoming advocates for them, youth pastors and leaders actualize the love of God in Jesus Christ for the world.

Conclusion

The current crisis of young people, faith, and the church is a complex, emotionally charged issue. It involves parents, family members, and friends who love their children and who are concerned about their spiritual and faith life. I have experienced this firsthand in the writing of this book. Time after time colleagues and friends would ask about the topic, and when I would tell them it deals with young people leaving the church, I would hear stories, sometimes accompanied by tears, from parents mourning the fact that their kids no longer "go to church." These heartfelt responses show there are no easy solutions to this issue; there is no magic theory that will adequately address all the issues discussed above.

Rather than trying to solve the "problem" of young people the Christian community can and should take practical steps to reexamine the life of the community in the context of the gospel. Any conversation about "faith" must begin with a definition: What does it mean to believe? This leads to a thick description of Christian faith: Who or what do we believe in? This

—CONCLUSION—

conversation draws attention to the purpose and nature of the Christian community in which faith is central, which leads to the fundamental question: What does it mean to be the church?

The answers to these questions are derived from the Christian tradition: from Scripture, confessions, doctrine, and Christian practice. But these sources must always be brought into dialogue with the lived experiences of individuals and communities, specifically focusing upon their cultural and social contexts. It is this process of dialogue in which the dialectic of "narration" and "renarration" must take place as Christian identity, and what it means to be the church both in and for the world, is negotiated and renegotiated.

Theologically, the community must reflect upon God's action in Jesus Christ, and what it means for the crucified and risen Christ to be the object of Christian faith. However, it is important to recognize the social and cultural forces at work in the lives of young people that shape the social imaginary by which they construct identity. It is within the tension of this dialectic, the revelation of God in Jesus Christ, and the social and cultural experience of young people, that this specific issue of young people and faith must be discussed.

The purpose of this discussion has been to bring together the insights of Charles Taylor and Dietrich Bonhoeffer as two representatives of this dialectic. Charles Taylor's work helps frame the social imaginary of young people, providing an important context for understanding the pervasive influence of Moral Therapeutic Deism and the tension that exists between the world of young people in the West and the Christian tradition. The theology of Dietrich Bonhoeffer provides insight into the sociality of faith and what it means to believe in the crucified and risen Christ. Bonhoeffer also provides a definition of the church grounded in God's love for humanity and the world, in which the church is understood to be the actualization of the new humanity—the humanity of the crucified and resurrected Christ—in history.

Ultimately, Bonhoeffer provides a theological paradigm from which the Christian community can affirm the humanity of young people, push back against the cultural narrative of global technocapitalism and the consumer society that abstracts and fragments their lives, and help foster a poetic renarration of identity in the context of the death and resurrection of Jesus Christ. It is in the context of this tension between the revelation of God in Jesus Christ and the cultural experience of young people that the

Christian community must take responsibility for the humanity of young people by entering their lived experience in order to communicate and perform the new humanity of the resurrected Christ.

Bibliography

Arnett, Jeffrey Jensen. *Emerging Adulthood: The Winding Road from the Late Teens through the Twenties*. New York: Oxford University Press, 2004.
Arthur, Sarah. *The God-Hungry Imagination: The Art of Storytelling for Postmodern Youth Ministry*. Nashville: Upper Room, 2007.
Barber, Benjamin R. *Consumed: How Markets Corrupt Children, Infantilize Adults, and Swallow Citizens Whole*. New York: W. W. Norton, 2007.
Barna Group. "Six Reasons Young Christians Leave the Church." http://www.barna.org/teens-next-gen-articles/528-six-reasons-young-christians-leave-church.
Bauman, Zygmunt. *Consuming Life*. Malden, MA: Polity, 2007.
———. *Globalization: The Human Consequences*. European Perspectives. New York: Columbia University Press, 1998.
Bell, Daniel. *The Coming of Post-Industrial Society*. New York: Basic, 1973.
Blumenberg, Hans. *The Legitimacy of the Modern Age*. Studies in Contemporary German Social Thought. Cambridge: MIT Press, 1983.
Bonhoeffer, Dietrich. *Act and Being: Transcendental Philosophy and Ontology in Systematic Theology*. Vol. 2, Dietrich Bonhoeffer Works. English ed. Translated by H. Martin Rumscheidt. Minneapolis: Fortress, 2009.
———. *Conspiracy and Imprisonment, 1940–1945*. Vol. 16, Dietrich Bonhoeffer Works. English ed. Edited by Mark S. Brocker. Translated by Lisa E. Dahill with the assistance of Douglas W. Stott. Minneapolis: Fortress, 2006.
———. *Creation and Fall: A Theological Exposition of Genesis 1–3*. Vol. 3, Dietrich Bonhoeffer Works. English ed. Translated by John W. De Gruchy and Douglas S. Bax. Minneapolis: Fortress, 1997.
———. *Discipleship*. Vol. 4, Dietrich Bonhoeffer Works. English ed. Translated by Barbara Green and Reinhard Krauss. Minneapolis: Fortress, 2001.
———. *A Testament to Freedom: The Essential Writings of Dietrich Bonhoeffer*. Rev. ed. Edited by Geffrey B. Kelly and F. Burton Nelson. San Francisco: HarperSanFrancisco, 1995.
———. *Ethics*. Vol. 6, Dietrich Bonhoeffer Works. English ed. Translated by Reinhard Krauss, Charles C. West, and Douglas W. Scott. Minneapolis: Fortress, 2005.
———. *Letters and Papers from Prison*. Vol. 8, Dietrich Bonhoeffer Works. English ed. Edited by Christian Gremmels et. al. Translated by Isabel Best et. al. Minneapolis: Fortress, 2010.

—BIBLIOGRAPHY—

———. *Sanctorum Communio: A Theological Study of the Sociology of the Church.* Vol. 1, Dietrich Bonhoeffer Works. English ed. Translated by Reinhard Krauss and Nancy Lukens. Minneapolis: Fortress, 1998.
Brown, Stuart L., and Christopher C. Vaughan. *Play: How It Shapes the Brain, Opens the Imagination, and Invigorates the Soul.* New York: Avery, 2009.
Caputo, John D. *The Weakness of God: A Theology of the Event.* Indiana Series in the Philosophy of Religion. Bloomington, IN: Indiana University Press, 2006.
———. *What Would Jesus Deconstruct?: The Good News of Postmodernism for the Church.* The Church and Postmodern Culture. Grand Rapids: Baker Academic, 2007.
Certeau, Michel de. *The Practice of Everyday Life.* Berkeley, CA: University of California Press, 1984.
Clark, Chap. *Hurt 2.0: Inside the World of Today's Teenagers.* Youth, Family, and Culture. Grand Rapids: Baker Academic, 2011.
Columbus, Chris, director. *Harry Potter and the Sorcerer's Stone.* 152 mn. Warner Bros., 2001.
Dean, Kenda Creasy. *Almost Christian: What the Faith of Our Teenagers Is Telling the American Church.* New York: Oxford University Press, 2010.
Dumas, Andrâe. *Dietrich Bonhoeffer, Theologian of Reality.* New York: Macmillan, 1971.
Fisher, Eran. "The Classless Workplace: The Digeratie and the New Spirit of Technocapitalism." *Working USA: The Journal of Labor and Society* 11, no. 2 (2008) 181–98.
Foucault, Michel. *Discipline and Punish: The Birth of the Prison.* 2nd Vintage Books ed. New York: Vintage, 1995.
———. *The Essential Foucault: Selections from Essential Works of Foucault, 1954–1984.* Edited by Paul Rabinow and Nikolas S. Rose. New York: New Press, 2003.
Gallup, George, Jr. "The Religiosity Cycle." http://www.gallup.com/poll/6124/religiosity-cycle.aspx.
Gerkin, Charles V. *An Introduction to Pastoral Care.* Nashville: Abingdon, 1997.
Giroux, Henry A. *Youth in a Suspect Society: Democracy or Disposability?* New York: Palgrave Macmillan, 2009.
Goodchild, Philip. *Theology of Money.* New Slant: Religion, Politics, Ontology. Durham, NC: Duke University Press, 2009.
Green, Clifford J. *Bonhoeffer: A Theology of Sociality.* Rev. ed. Grand Rapids: Eerdmans, 1999.
Gregor, Brian, and Jens Zimmermann, eds. *Bonhoeffer and Continental Thought: Cruciform Philosophy.* Indiana Series in the Philosophy of Religion. Bloomington: Indiana University Press, 2009.
Hardt, Michael, and Antonio Negri. *Empire.* Cambridge: Harvard University Press, 2000.
Hill, Jonathan P. "Faith and Understanding: Specifying the Impact of Higher Education on Religious Belief." *Journal for the Scientific Study of Religion* 50, no. 3 (2011) 533–51.
Holland, Scott. "First We Take Manhattan, Then We Take Berlin: Bonhoeffer's New York." *CrossCurrents*, no. 3 (2000). http://www.crosscurrents.org/hollandf20.htm.
Jones, Serene. *Feminist Theory and Christian Theology: Cartographies of Grace.* Guides to Theological Inquiry. Minneapolis: Fortress, 2000.
———. *Trauma and Grace: Theology in a Ruptured World.* Louisville: Westminster John Knox, 2009.
Johnson, Byron, and Rodney Stark. "Religion and the Bad News Bearers: The Widely Reported Decline in Women's Church Attendance is Implausible." *The Wall Street*

Journal Online, August 26, 2011. http://www.wsj.com/articles/SB10000142405311190348090457651069269173491 6.

Kearney, G. R. *More Than a Dream: The Cristo Rey Story—How One School's Vision Is Changing the World*. Chicago: Loyola, 2008.

Kinnaman, David, and Aly Hawkins. *You Lost Me: Why Young Christians Are Leaving Church—and Rethinking Faith*. Grand Rapids: Baker, 2011.

Lawrence, Rick. *Jesus-Centered Youth Ministry*. Loveland, CO: Group, 2007.

Lief, Jason. "Some Kind of Monstrosity: What Youth Ministry Can Learn from Heavy Metal." *Journal of Youth and Theology* 13, no. 2 (2013) 7–22.

LifeWay Research. "Church Dropouts: How Many Leave Church between Ages 18–22 and Why?" http://liveabove.com/documents/research/Part_1_Church_Dropouts_How Many_Leave_Church_and_Why.pdf.

Löwith, Karl. *Meaning in History: The Theological Implications of the Philosophy of History*. Chicago: University of Chicago Press, 1949.

Marsh, Charles. *Reclaiming Dietrich Bonhoeffer: The Promise of His Theology*. New York: Oxford University Press, 1994.

Martinson, Roland D., Wesley Black, and John Roberto. *The Spirit and Culture of Youth Ministry: Leading Congregations toward Exemplary Youth Ministry*. St. Paul: EYM, 2010.

Moltmann, Jürgen. *God in Creation: A New Theology of Creation and the Spirit of God*. Minneapolis: Fortress, 1993.

Mueller, Walt. *Youth Culture 101*. Grand Rapids: Youth Specialties, 2007.

The National Study of Youth and Religion. http://www.youthandreligion.org.

Neuger, Christie Cozad. *Counseling Women: A Narrative, Pastoral Approach*. Minneapolis: Fortress, 2001.

Ott, Heinrich. *Reality and Faith: The Theological Legacy of Dietrich Bonhoeffer*. Philadelphia: Fortress, 1972.

The Pew Forum on Religion and Public Life. "'Nones' on the Rise: One in Five Adults Have No Religious Affiliation." http://www.pewforum.org/2012/10/09/nones-on-the-rise/.

Phillips, John A. *Christ for Us in the Theology of Dietrich Bonhoeffer*. New York: Harper and Row, 1967.

———. *The Form of Christ in the World: A Study of Bonhoeffer's Christology*. London: Collins, 1967.

Powell, Kara Eckmann, and Chap Clark. *Sticky Faith: Everyday Ideas to Build Lasting Faith in Your Kids*. Grand Rapids: Zondervan, 2011.

Reid, Alvin L. *Raising the Bar: Ministry to Youth in the New Millennium*. Grand Rapids: Kregel, 2004.

Ricoeur, Paul. *The Rule of Metaphor: Multi-Disciplinary Studies of the Creation of Meaning in Language*. University of Toronto Romance Series. Toronto: University of Toronto Press, 1977.

Ricoeur, Paul, and Mark I. Wallace. *Figuring the Sacred: Religion, Narrative, and Imagination*. Minneapolis: Fortress, 1995.

Robbins, Duffy. *Building a Youth Ministry That Builds Disciples: A Small Book About a Big Idea*. Grand Rapids: Zondervan, 2011.

Root, Andrew, and Kenda Creasy Dean. *The Theological Turn in Youth Ministry*. Downers Grove, IL: InterVarsity, 2011.

—Bibliography—

Rose, Tricia. *The Hip Hop Wars: What We Talk About When We Talk About Hip Hop—and Why It Matters*. New York: Basic Civitas, 2008.
Senter, Mark. *Four Views of Youth Ministry and the Church: Inclusive Congregational, Preparatory, Missional, Strategic*. Grand Rapids: Youth Specialties, 2001.
Smedes, Lewis B. *Sex for Christians: The Limits and Liberties of Sexual Living*. Rev. ed. Grand Rapids: Eerdmans, 1994.
Smith, Christian, Kari Marie Christoffersen, Hilary Davidson, and Patricia Snell Herzog. *Lost in Transition: The Dark Side of Emerging Adulthood*. New York: Oxford University Press, 2011.
Smith, Christian, and Melinda Lundquist Denton. *Soul Searching: The Religious and Spiritual Lives of American Teenagers*. New York: Oxford University Press, 2005.
Smith, Christian, and Patricia Snell. *Souls in Transition: The Religious and Spiritual Lives of Emerging Adults*. New York: Oxford University Press, 2009.
Stanton, Andrew, director. *WALL-E*. Walt Disney Studios, 2008.
Suarez-Villa, Luis. *Globalization and Technocapitalism: The Political Economy of Corporate Power and Technological Domination*. Burlington, VT: Ashgate, 2012.
———. *Invention and the Rise of Technocapitalism*. Lanham, MD: Rowman and Littlefield, 2000.
———. *Technocapitalism: A Critical Perspective on Technological Innovation and Corporatism*. Philadelphia: Temple University Press, 2009.
Taylor, Charles. *A Secular Age*. Cambridge: Harvard University Press, 2007.
———. *Sources of the Self: The Making of the Modern Identity*. Cambridge: Harvard University Press, 1989.
Turpin, Katherine. *Branded: Adolescents Converting from Consumer Faith*. Youth Ministry Alternatives. Cleveland: Pilgrim, 2006.
Vattimo, Gianni. *After Christianity*. Italian Academy Lectures. New York: Columbia University Press, 2002.
White, David F. *Practicing Discernment with Youth: A Transformative Youth Ministry Approach*. Youth Ministry Alternatives. Cleveland: Pilgrim, 2005.
White, Michael, and David Epston. *Narrative Means to Therapeutic Ends*. New York: Norton, 1990.
Wolin, Sheldon S. *Democracy Incorporated: Managed Democracy and the Specter of Inverted Totalitarianism*. Princeton, NJ: Princeton University Press, 2008.
Wright, Bradley R. *Christians Are Hate-Filled Hypocrites—and Other Lies You've Been Told: A Sociologist Shatters Myths from the Secular and Christian Media*. Minneapolis: Bethany House, 2010.
Zimmermann, Jens, and Brian Gregor. *Being Human, Becoming Human: Dietrich Bonhoeffer and Social Thought*. Eugene, OR: Pickwick, 2010.
Žižek, Slavoj. *The Fragile Absolute, or, Why Is the Christian Legacy Worth Fighting For?* Wo Es War. New York: Verso, 2000.
Žižek, Slavoj, John Milbank. *The Monstrosity of Christ: Paradox or Dialectic?* Edited by Creston Davis Short Circuits. Cambridge: MIT Press, 2009.

Index

Bauman, Zygmunt, 57–62, 65, 67, 74, 119, 122, 143
   consumer society, 58–63, 65–66, 68, 72, 74, 90, 91, 96, 102–3, 107, 118–19, 122, 124–27, 139
   failed consumer, 60, 65
Bonhoeffer, Dietrich, 16, 70, 78–107, 109–10, 112, 114–16, 121, 126, 134–35, 141, 143–46
   Act and Being, 92, 142
   Adam—80, 85, 92
   "After Ten Years", 81
   church, 70, 79, 81, 84, 88, 91, 94–102, 104–5, 107–8, 114, 116, 141
   Creation and Fall, 92, 143
   Deus ex machina, 79, 107
   Discipleship, 85, 105, 115, 143
   Ethics, 79, 83, 115, 143
   faith, 80, 82, 84, 88, 92, 101–2, 105–6, 116
   Letters and Papers From Prison, 78, 99, 115, 143
   new humanity, 16, 85, 90, 92, 94–95, 97–98, 102, 105, 110, 116, 135, 141–42
   religion, 73–75, 79–81, 83–84, 94–96, 102, 107, 110, 126
   responsibility, 16, 81–84, 86, 95, 98–100, 102–3, 105, 116, 120, 135
   Sanctorum Communio, 81, 94, 144
Brown, Stuart, 127, 144
Bultmann, Rudolph, 109–10

Caputo, John D., 15–16, 24–25, 108–9, 144
   theo-poetics, 108–9
   weak theology, 29–30, 86–87, 122
Certeau, Michel de, 113–14, 138, 144
Clark, Chap, 4–5, 10–11, 20–23, 144–45
College Transition Study, 10
Cristo Rey, 139–40, 145

Dean, Kenda Creasy, 7–8, 10, 134, 144–45
demythologization, 109–10

emergent adulthood, 6, 8, 11, 30, 66–67

Foucault, Michel, 16, 32, 35, 41–44, 56, 63–64, 144
   pastoral power-16, 35, 41–44, 64
   disciplinary society, 35, 41–42

Gerkin, Charles, 120, 144
Giroux, Henry, 61–62, 67, 119, 144
Goodchild, Phillip, 45–47, 53, 107, 144

Hardt, Michael, 63–65, 144

Jones, Serene, 121, 130, 144

Kinnaman, David, 4, 9–10, 23, 100–101, 118, 145

Lawrence, Rick, 20–21

Moltmann, Jürgen, 127, 145
Moral Therapeutic Deism, 5–8, 12, 16, 26–27, 35, 40, 53–54, 66, 69, 90–91, 118–19, 141
National Study of Youth and Religion, 5–7, 145
narrative therapy, 124
Negri, Antonio, 63–65, 144
Neuger, Christie Cozad, 132–33, 145

Pew Forum on Religion and Public Life, 3
play, 106, 127–28, 144
poetic, 16, 18, 91, 108–13, 115, 119–23, 126–27, 129, 131, 133–37, 141
Powell, Kara, 4–5, 10–11, 23, 145

remythologization, 16, 91, 110, 112, 121
renarration, 120, 124–25, 133, 136, 141
Ricoeur, Paul, 110–12, 120, 145

social imaginary, 12–13, 16, 29, 33, 35–41, 43–48, 52, 54–57, 60, 63–64, 66, 69, 82, 85, 90–91, 96, 104, 118–19, 141
Smith, Christian, 5–7, 10–11, 30–31, 40, 53, 67, 90, 118, 146

Sticky Faith, 4–5, 10–11, 22–23, 118, 145
Suarez-Villa, Luis, 13, 49–51, 53, 146

Taylor, Charles, 16, 29–30, 32, 34–40, 43–44, 46–49, 52–53, 57, 63, 74, 107, 141, 146
  immanent frame, 38–41
  secularity, 34–35, 40, 43–44, 46–47, 52–53
  The Secular Age, 29, 34–35, 44
  Sources of the Self, 43, 146
Technocapitalism, 14–16, 26–28, 32–35, 49–52, 54, 56–57, 60–61, 63–65, 66, 68–70, 82, 84, 90, 103, 107, 113, 115–16, 118–21, 127, 137–39, 141, 144, 146

Vattimo, Gianni, 15–16, 25–26, 43, 52, 146
  weak thought, 29

White, Michael, 124–25, 146

Žižek, Slovoj, 73, 75–78, 82, 85
  monstrosity, 75–78, 82, 85, 146
  The Fragile Absolute, 77–78, 146

www.ingramcontent.com/pod-product-compliance
Lightning Source LLC
Chambersburg PA
CBHW022121160426
43197CB00009B/1113